Critical Guides to Spanish and Latin American Texts and Films

74 Laura Esquivel: Como agua para chocolate,
    The Novel and Film Version

Critical Guides to Spanish and Latin American Texts and Films

EDITED BY ALAN DEYERMOND & STEPHEN HART

Como agua para chocolate,
The Novel and Film Version

Nathanial Gardner

Lecturer in Latin American Studies
University of Glasgow

Grant & Cutler Ltd
2009

ISBN: 9780729304535

Printed in Spain by
Artes Gráficas Soler, S. L., Valencia
for
GRANT & CUTLER LTD
55–57 GREAT MARLBOROUGH STREET, LONDON W1F 7AY

Contents

Prefatory Note

This critical guide will be roughly divided into two sections: the first half deals with the novel and the second takes on the film. However, due to the great similarity of each — probably, in some respects, owing to the fact that both the author and the scriptwriter are the same person — there is a fair amount of overlap. References to the film are made in the section on the novel and vice-versa. Likewise, sections such as themes (which are found in the novel half of the guide) will mostly apply to the film as well. All page references which do not have a reference number with them, should be assumed to be from the 1992 Doubleday edition of *Como agua* and, unless otherwise indicated, all translations should be viewed as the author's. Great efforts were made to obtain permission to use the stills from the film, but it proved impossible to establish contact with the copyright holder. The publisher would be happy to make the appropriate acknowledgements in any future edition.

Introduction

Laura Esquivel

Born in Mexico City in 1950, Laura Esquivel entered the world of writing as a scriptwriter. Esquivel has commented that her most famous novel, *Como agua para chocolate,*[1] was originally conceived as the screenplay for a film. However, when she tried to convince producers to make the film she was discouraged due to the high cost of creating a 'period film'. A novel, it was decided, would be a more appropriate medium for the story (*45*, no pagination) and so she wrote one, publishing it in 1989. It was an immediate success, with a huge number of people being smitten by the mixture of love, betrayal, passion and cooking. The novel quickly became a national, and then an international, bestseller. Ironically, the story was then contemplated as a film. Esquivel wrote the screenplay for the film and her then husband, Alfonso Arau, produced and directed it. This also accounts for the fact that the film version is exceptionally faithful to the original book. It has even been noted that the novel reads like a screenplay (*5*, p.174). This would seem logical given the author's comments on its construction. Like the novel, the film was an enormous success. After its subtitled release in the USA in February 1993, by June of the same year it 'had grossed 6.1 million dollars, the highest box office receipts ever for a Latin American film released in the United States' (*26*, p.45). By September 1993 'the film continued to show 'tremendous legs', with a box office gross of over $17 million' (*26*, p.45), making it a huge success in the world of film and literature. It has even been suggested that it was the film's enormous success which opened the way for the great increase in the

---

[1] From this point forward the title, *Como agua para chocolate*, will simply be referred to as *Como agua*.

number of Spanish language films to be found on the international film market today (*8*, no pagination). Indeed, both the reading and the film public continue to be enchanted by its romantic and turbulent story.

Though some critics have slighted Esquivel's narrative (*11*, pp.66–67), the film version was acclaimed. It took eleven of the prestigious Ariel awards (Mexico's highest film awards) the year it was released, and was awarded many others for its excellence at locations such as the Guadalajara Mexican Film Festival, the Sudbury Cinéfest, the Tokyo International Film Festival and the Independent Spirit Awards. In addition to these honours, *Como agua* was also nominated for awards in prestigious circles such as the BAFTA Awards, the Goya Awards and the Golden Globes. So, whilst some critics may have criticised Arau's and Esquivel's work as 'crowd pleasing', it is also true that top award-granting bodies were also well aware of the film's significance.

Plot summary of the novel

Tita De la Garza is born on a Mexican ranch near Eagle Pass, Texas, at the turn of the twentieth century. Receiving bad news just after Tita's birth, Juan De la Garza, Tita's father, dies of a heart attack. His widow, Mamá Elena De la Garza, is left to raise her three daughters, Rosaura, Gertrudis and Josefita (Tita), with the help of her servants — especially Nacha and Chencha. Early on we learn that Tita will not be allowed to marry or leave the ranch owing to a family tradition which obliges the youngest daughter to take care of her mother until she dies. As she is about to turn sixteen, Pedro Muzquiz comes to the De la Garza home to ask for Tita's hand in marriage but, because of the family tradition, he is offered Rosaura's hand in marriage instead. He accepts the offer in order to live near Tita — his true love. Rosaura and Pedro are married, but Tita's crying into the batter of the wedding cake precipitates a magical event which causes everyone who eats it to feel nostalgic for the love of their life, and then to vomit. Nacha, the first to try the cake, dies from its effects.

After her mentor/surrogate mother's death, Tita takes over Nacha's place as the head cook of the ranch. One year later, as a result of the aphrodisiacal effects of a meal made from roses which Tita has prepared, Gertrudis runs off with a soldier from the Mexican revolution. Mamá Elena burns her middle daughter's photos and birth certificate after hearing that Gertrudis is working in a brothel, and forbids anyone from mentioning her name. Rosaura has her baby, but Tita breastfeeds him. Mamá Elena suspects (correctly) a romance between Tita and Pedro and sends Rosaura and Pedro to San Antonio, Texas. While there, Rosaura's baby dies from feeding complications. This sad news drives Tita insane and her mother orders the family doctor, Dr Brown, to take her to an asylum. Dr Brown takes her to his home instead. Chencha cures Tita with the help of soup and Dr Brown falls in love with her. Tita accepts Dr Brown's wedding proposal. Bandits attack the De la Garza ranch, rape Chencha and wound Mamá Elena in such a way as to make her dependent on Tita's care. Tita returns to the ranch to watch over her mother but, due to medical complications, her mother dies soon after.

Rosaura and Pedro return to the family home after Mamá Elena's death. Esperanza, Rosaura's second and last child, is born. Rosaura announces that she plans to continue the family tradition of keeping her youngest daughter as a personal carer. Dr Brown and Tita formalise their relationship. Pedro traps Tita in an abandoned shed on the ranch and makes love to her for the first time. Tita believes she is pregnant. Gertrudis returns to the ranch for a visit. She is now married to Juan Alejandrez, and is a *generala* commanding troops in the Mexican revolution. After advice from Gertrudis, Tita tells Pedro she believes she is pregnant. Pedro is overjoyed and proposes that they escape from the ranch. Tita rejects the idea and soon after learns that she is not pregnant after all. Rosaura confronts Tita about her affair with Pedro. Tita confesses, but reproaches her for having stolen Pedro in the first place.

Tita, fearing Dr Brown will not want her after losing her virginity to Pedro, confesses to him that she is no longer a virgin, scared that he will no longer want to marry her. The doctor proclaims his enduring love for Tita and assures her that, if she wishes, he is still willing to marry her.

The narrative then leaps approximately twenty years into the future. We discover that Tita never married Dr John Brown after all. Rosaura has recently passed away and Esperanza is to marry Alex Brown, Dr Brown's son. Pedro proposes to Tita and she accepts. All appear to be content — except for Dr Brown, who is presumably disappointed at losing the chance to marry Tita. After a wonderful wedding and reception, Pedro and Tita make love in the shed where they had their first sexual experience and their passion is so great that they die as a result of their love making and the whole ranch bursts into flames.

Part One: The novel

1. Characters

There are eight main characters and seven secondary characters in *Como agua* who appear in the majority of the scenes in both the novel and the film. I will briefly describe them, their role in the narrative/film, as well as provide important considerations about each individual.

(Josefita) Tita

The youngest of the three daughters, Tita was born to Mamá Elena De la Garza and Señor Juan De la Garza. Her father dies soon after her birth — because someone suggests that his middle child, Gertrudis, was sired by Mamá Elena's mulatto lover. Tita is practically raised in the kitchen by the ranch's cook Nacha. There, Tita acquires a love for all things related to the culinary arts, in which she herself is incredibly gifted. She is seen as having a sixth sense for cooking that can be viewed as both a blessing and a curse. She is even described as being the last link in a chain of pre-Hispanic cooks who have passed on culinary secrets from generation to generation (p.47). As the youngest daughter, Tita is obliged to refrain from marrying or having children, and is forced to take care of her mother until her death. Though in love with Pedro Muzquiz (and he with her), they are forbidden to marry — as a compromise Pedro marries Tita's sister Rosaura in order to be close to Tita —though they do eventually become lovers. Tita is often seen as alone and isolated in the novel; something she believes has been brought about, at least in part, by Mamá Elena's special requirements. However, Tita is characterised as being a person who is balanced precariously between rebelliousness, and submissiveness to family traditions. Even though she has moments when she does defy her mother,

ultimately she is obedient to her wish that she should deny herself
marriage (and, ultimately, sexuality) until after her mother's death.
The novel depicts Tita as being physically voluptuous.

Pedro

The son of Pascual Muzquiz, Pedro is Tita's first and only lasting
love in *Como agua*. Little is divulged in the novel about his
schooling or family; however, his surname seems to suggest a
possible connection with, or reference to, the Kickapoo Indian tribe,
as those Indians settled in a town named Muzquiz in Coahuila,
Mexico (*41*, pp. 19–20). Likewise, the novel reveals that he speaks
English perfectly and is qualified to work as an accountant. After
swearing eternal love to Tita, Pedro's marriage to Rosaura allows
him to share the same house as her. Essentially, Pedro is portrayed,
as I shall show below, as a castrated male — thus he allows Mamá
Elena to dictate whom he will marry, where he will live and what his
livelihood will be — and his mother-in-law continually denies the
fulfilment of his wishes. Only after her death does he dare to initiate
sexual relations with Tita. Towards the end of the novel, after Mamá
Elena's death, he does adopt a more machista role, initiating a sexual
relationship with Tita and making her 'perder la virginidad y conocer
el verdadero amor' (p.159). The character finds great pleasure in the
idea of having a child with Tita. Although he does promise eternal
love to her, he is ultimately a coward. Throughout the narrative, he
never confronts any of his enemies/rivals directly and only ever
demonstrates his love through secret approaches.

Mamá Elena De la Garza

Portrayed as a strong matriarch, Mamá Elena rules her ranch, and
those who live on it, with an iron hand. Mamá Elena sees no need for
men and does not remarry after Juan's death, nor is she seen to
consider romantic relationships. She has been compared to the
controlling mother in García Lorca's famous play *La casa de
Bernarda Alba* (*15*, no pagination). Mamá Elena, in the name of
'decency' and old-fashioned values, dictates how people will act.

Though the narrator does show us that she has her weaknesses (she too cries under the magical spell of the cake at Rosaura's wedding) and can be hypocritical (after being forbidden to marry a mulatto Mexican, she maintains an adulterous relationship with him and bears him a child — her second daughter Gertrudis). Mamá Elena appears to feed off the need to control her daughters and, in one of the novel's nods to magic realism, even continues to haunt Tita after her death.

Rosaura

Mamá Elena and Señor Juan De la Garza's eldest daughter, Rosaura, could be seen as a woman caught between tradition and love — family and societal tradition, and the love that exists between Tita and Pedro. She enters into a marriage contract with Pedro because her mother arranges it. Like her two sisters, she appears unable to defy her mother (she accepts marriage to her sister's boyfriend without protest); Rosaura also appears unable to stand up to her husband when he becomes unfaithful (as long as society does not find out about his infidelity she is willing to continue with such an arrangement). Her acceptance of this relationship is probably due to guilt at depriving Pedro of Tita's love. Both Rosaura and Gertrudis appear to be magically affected by Tita's food (Gertrudis becomes sexually aroused by it on one occasion). Rosaura finds that Tita's food physically deforms her — she becomes seriously overweight. She also suffers from bad halitosis, as well as terrible bouts of flatulence, both caused by eating, and which ultimately cause her death.

Gertrudis

The fruit of an illegitimate relationship between Mamá Elena and her mulatto lover, José Treviño, Gertrudis is a stereotypical character. She is portrayed as sexually aggressive — she goes away to live in a whorehouse because she was wearing out the man she was with. She possesses an innate ability with regard to dance and rhythm — a trait, we learn, that she has inherited from her father. Her ease for copying rhythm is implied only in the film and, in the novel, she is merely described as having large breasts. She is portrayed as non-mulatto; this we know because her husband is surprised when their son is born with mulatto features; and in the film she is the fairest of the three. She is portrayed as the only member of the family who is able to understand Tita. Gertrudis is the most domineering of the three. After eating the aphrodisiacal meal prepared by Tita, which has magical effects on her, she runs away from home with a soldier of the Mexican Revolution, becomes a prostitute, and, later, a respected *generala* in the Mexican Revolution. Eventually she becomes a wife and mother. Apparently the one with the most control over her life and desires, her dominance is assured after leaving the De la Garza Ranch.

Juan Alejandrez

This general in the Mexican Revolution is the man who leads Gertrudis away from her family ranch and initiates her sexually (though she later abandons him when he cannot fulfil her needs). After her time as a prostitute, Juan and Gertrudis meet again, fight together in the army, marry and eventually have a child. While portrayed as very masculine, the character defies the 'macho' stereotype in many ways. He admits his lack of virility to Gertrudis, and later accepts her after she has been with many others. On several occasions, he allows his will to bend to his spouse's.

Nacha

Though she dies in the second chapter of the novel (soon after partaking of Rosaura's wedding cake), her character appears sporadically throughout the novel. She is portrayed as Tita's spiritual and culinary guide, as well as her only intimate friend and mother figure. Though illiterate, Nacha is an expert in the culinary arts, and in other areas such as folk remedies. This lack of education, mixed with wisdom acquired in life, is demonstrated by her sound advice in a very uneducated Spanish. Nacha's death transforms her into the equivalent of a saint or guardian angel. Tita prays to her, is visited by her, and receives her down-to-earth advice on several occasions.

Chencha

The other household servant in the De la Garza home, Chencha, is from the lower substratum of Mexican society. She is also poorly educated; this is portrayed by her speech though, unlike Nacha, she is not endowed with popular wisdom. She simply has a happy-go-lucky attitude — apparently oblivious to the important events occurring around her; she is a kind of 'noble savage'. Though raped by revolutionary soldiers, she later marries her first love and returns to the ranch with plans to have many children, 'living happily every after' (p.152).

Dr Brown

The De la Garza family doctor is timid and serious-minded, but open in his world view. He is, for example, willing to marry Tita for love, even though she has been unfaithful to him during their engagement. While he is a man of science, shown in his medical practice and in his knowledge of other areas of science such as chemistry, he is also depicted as open to alternative or non-scientific explanations and avenues of research (for example his grandmother's research into the medicinal properties of the Tepezcohuite plant). In particular he has the idea that we all have a box of matches within us, which can be ignited by love's touch. Ultimately though, he stays on the northern side of the US/Mexican border and, although the narrative does not show this overtly, as Alex's father and Esperanza's father-in-law he quietly becomes the patriarch of the De la Garza descendants.

Sargento Treviño

One of Gertrudis' subordinates, Sargento Treviño is one of the leading soldiers in her battalion. He is portrayed as a semi-literate man who helps Gertrudis, even with cooking. His role as a comical figure is much more apparent in the film than it is in the novel.

Father Ignacio

The De la Garza family's Catholic priest, he performs the weddings, funerals, baptisms, and other religious functions required by the family. He is also the object of subtle religious criticism when he explains that he found that Gertrudis was working in a brothel on the border — it is implied that he discovered this information as a result of a personal visit to the house of ill repute. This type of misbehaviour is underlined in the film when he is seen running off — presumably to have sex — with the neighbourhood busybody, Paquita Lobo.

Paquita Lobo

The source of local gossip, yet always invited to every event, Paquita is a humorous addition to the major events in *Como agua*. Her comments are always designed to solicit new gossip about the moral transgressions of the region's inhabitants, while portraying herself as above her neighbours' follies. In the film, she falls from her 'holier-than-thou' pedestal when she is seen leaving a social event with the local priest.

Esperanza

Esperanza is Pedro and Rosaura's only daughter. Though originally to be named Tita (an allusion to the fact that Rosaura wanted her to carry on the family tradition of not being allowed to marry in order to take care of her mother) Rosaura is persuaded to name her Esperanza — 'hope' — a clear indication that she will bring about the demise of the restrictive family tradition. This she does when she marries Alex. She is described as being very feminine (p.240).

Alex

Dr John Brown's son, Alex, decides he will marry Esperanza early on in the novel — though this is initially prohibited by Rosaura. However, after his mother-in-law-to-be dies, no one opposes him. He carries on a Brown family tradition in marrying someone who is not a mainstream American (just like his great-great-grandfather, who married a Kickapoo Indian, and just like his father who intended to marry Tita) though this time it is done with his family's approval. He is essentially seen as a progressive gringo who, according to most, is 'el mejor partido [...] en 10 millas a la redonda' (p.241) and who takes Esperanza from a small ranch in northern Mexico to Harvard University with him.

2. Themes

Rebellion vs. Tradition

In many ways *Como agua* is about tradition. It is true that, before the Mexican Revolution, societal tradition dictated many of the ways in which women lived, both in rural and urban Mexico. Women were taught to read and write and, if they were of indigenous origin, to speak Spanish in segregated schools — the segregation dependent not only upon sex, but upon race as well (*35*, pp.9 & 20). At school they were taught 'to be submissive, modest, quiet, and well-bathed' as well as to have 'manners and good taste' (*49*, p.68). Religious piety and 'work appropriate for their sex', such as sewing, patching, drawing patterns, cutting, embroidering and knitting, also formed an integral part of formal education for many (*49*, pp.99 & 183–186). While public life, as suggested by a painting of the period, did exist on some level — often in the form of street vendors, or aristocracy out on a stroll — it was limited, and the majority of women led lives mainly within the confines of their homes (*49*, p.53). However, notwithstanding the strict social constraints for women in pre-Revolutionary Mexico, it does not appear to be the case that the De la Garza 'youngest daughter takes care of the mother' tradition existed on any general level. Nonetheless, it is one of the main themes running though the narrative. The novel underlines the uniqueness of the theme with Dr Brown's surprised and critical reaction when Tita explains it to him: '¡Pero cómo! Eso es una tontería' (p.80). With the doctor's remark, Esquivel emphasises how absurd and unusual the tradition is. However Mamá Elena makes it clear on several occasions that the arrangement has existed within her family for a long time, and that her daughter will not be the one to break it. This is not the only tradition that the matriarch enforces. There are certain ways in which things have to be said: the idea that the children have to address their mother as *mami* because she does not like the way *mamá* sounds (something which helps to marginalise her daughters as *mami* is a term of address used by small children rather than adult daughters), or that when she says, 'Por hoy ya terminamos con esto' (p.8) it means that the day has effectively ended (for their household) and that everyone has to finish their activities.

There are other examples of tradition found on the De la Garza ranch. Some of them have to do with the relationship between husband and wife, like the ancient use of the *sábana nupcial*, which seems to mix biblical tradition (Deut. 22: 15–18) and prudishness as a means of creating a barrier between a married couple and to demonstrate virginity. Other examples underline the social boundaries in pre-Revolutionary Mexico which discourage the mixing of races and social classes (*40*, p.72 and *35*, p.9). The clearest example of this is Mamá Elena's being forbidden to form a relationship with a mulatto man, and his clandestine murder when the two try to carry out a plan to be together. Whilst Porfirio Díaz's *científicos* promoted the whitening of the Mexican population through 'European immigration, colonization' and formal and civic education (*47*, p.189), *Como agua*'s rhetoric appears to disapprove of what would be the darkening of a white Mexican family. Thus life is portrayed much more strictly: servants (who are always from the Mexican lower classes) marry servants, soldiers marry soldiers, and landed gentry marry those of their own social class. At least on the surface of the novel, society obeys very strict norms of social conduct which reflect the rigid hierarchy of pre-Revolutionary Mexican society.

In *Como agua*, even cooking implies tradition at a certain level. Indeed, the idea of a cookery book that is handed down from generation to generation (which, according to the narrator, Tita's grandniece, is the book we are reading) implies that meals, and the way of creating them, will be preserved and recreated as the family recreates itself in the future. The narrator thereby implies that the culinary traditions transmitted through the narrative offer a way in which Tita — or at least her memory — is able to live on into the future (p.242). However, in this area of tradition there appears to be more flexibility than in others. Foods are created 'out of season', as when *Tortas de Navidad* are made for Tita's birthday party instead of at Christmas, or *chocolate* and *Rosca de Reyes* (normally consumed on the 6th of January) are eaten in September. Despite the traditions, they are nonetheless prepared for special occasions, such as family parties, or for entertaining guests. Recipes are also permitted variations due to different circumstances, such as the use of quail instead of pheasant in Tita's special rose petal dish, when the traditional bird is unavailable.

Many of these seemingly small elements combine to depict a home that is steeped in tradition and which, unfortunately for many, is closed to the idea of change.

If, however, a major point of the narrative is the registering of tradition, much of the tension is produced by the subversion of tradition. Thus Tita describes the ways in which she and Pedro, when not allowed by tradition to marry, transgress 'norms of decency' and become lovers. Though they are not together in marriage, they are together at least in the flesh. Tita voices her displeasure with her family's tradition both to her mother 'Pero yo opino que no es justo' (p.9), and to Dr Brown 'Eso es una tontería. — Pero así es' (p.80) and she further underlines its injustice by explaining that it means that no one will be around to care for the youngest daughter (p.10). Mamá Elena sees her mulatto lover in secret, and even allows him to sire one of her children, illustrating her fundamental hypocrisy.

But these transgressions are, in many ways, merely digressions because, ultimately, the family tradition is upheld. When Mamá Elena plans to flee with her lover, unknown individuals kill him in the shadows and Mamá Elena returns to her husband's side for good. Tita and Pedro are only platonic/sentimental/voyeuristic lovers until Mamá Elena dies (and Tita is thereby conveniently freed from her duties to her mother), but they are not free from Pedro's marital duty to be a good husband, at least in the eyes of society. Rosaura, too, is compliant, agreeing to share her husband with Tita so long as her sister is discreet and she can remain the legitimate spouse. Rosaura's daughter, Esperanza, is freed from any obligation to care for her mother, and is allowed to marry Alex because, conveniently, her mother also dies before she reaches an appropriate age for marriage, though it is inferred that Pedro would have granted her permission to be married anyway. Nonetheless, Rosaura's death can be seen as a timely way of neatly resolving the conflict. Again, tradition is maintained due to convenient turns of events. Death is indeed a way in which *Como agua* successfully side-steps several conflicts, and could even be seen as a *Deus ex machina* technique, offering simple solutions to complicated human situations. Examples of these situations are abundant. Death prevents Mamá Elena from running off with her lover. Death allows Tita to be intimate with Pedro. Death allows Esperanza to marry Alex. Death also permits Dr Brown to become an eligible suitor for Tita (one imagines that had he simply been divorced, his status would have been different). Such simple solutions can be criticised (as *Deus ex machina* resolutions often are), but it could also be said that they add to the *telenovela* qualities of the novel, where quick and easy solutions to complicated dilemmas are ubiquitous. Sometimes departure rather than death is utilised. Esperanza appears to save her future children from any 'youngest daughter' obligations by her suggested emigration to the USA. Thus, the promise of the hope of escaping tradition is fulfilled by her mother's timely death and secured through crossing borders. Though some may argue that Pedro offers legitimacy to Tita at the beginning of their relationship — he does initially offer to marry her, and later to run away with her (when she suspects she is pregnant with Pedro's child) and finally offers to marry her once again when Esperanza marries Alex — in fact the wedding never takes place as the couple die first. Thus tradition is not broken, and, superficially at least, Mamá Elena's wish for Tita never to marry prevails. This has implications for an understanding of the novel, which portrays a conservative emotional ideology.

Whilst not bound to traditions of caring for her mother in the way that Tita and Esperanza are, Gertrudis is also an example of a non-traditional woman. After a magical episode linked to eating Tita's special quail in rose sauce, Gertrudis runs away from the ranch with a soldier of the Mexican Revolution and, not finding sexual satisfaction with him, she begins to work in a whorehouse. From a non-traditional exit from the ranch (as opposed to a traditional departure from the family home through marriage) she moves on to a non-traditional form of employment (as a prostitute). In time, she leaves the brothel for a more reputable form of employment, but not one usually chosen by women at that time: soldiering. The *soldadera*, whose name in Spanish denotes gendered difference from the male soldiers, was a woman of the Mexican Revolution who travelled with the fighting men and whose job 'was foraging, cooking and looking after the wounded', though it has been noted that they also 'pitched in and fought if they felt like it' (*44*, p.36). They were even given the option of inheriting their husband's uniform and gun if their partner was killed (*44*, p.36). It has been noted that most troops had *soldaderas*, and that their normal role was to feed the men; however, some did describe them as shameless, 'irredeemable concubines' (*44*, pp.36–37). Gertrudis is not a normal *soldadera*, however, and is soon a *generala*. While it is true that among the *Villista* troops at least one *generala*, Petra Herrera, did exist; it is also true that she had to disguise herself as 'Pedro Herrera' until she had demonstrated her excellent leadership qualities (*44*, p.48). This could well have been due to the fact that Pancho Villa had 'proved the most vehement hater of the *soldaderas*' (*44*, p.45) as he wanted his armies to mirror the more modern ones that existed, without *soldaderas*, in England and the USA. Given this, it would appear that Gertrudis' character has been exaggerated in several ways in order to portray her as an exceptional woman for her time. She does not appear to reject traditional femininity, but she does make significant progress in alternative professions and lifestyles for a woman in Mexico at the beginning of the twentieth century. Gertrudis is non-traditional in many ways, though there are episodes where she subverts gender roles, as when she orders one of her male subordinates to cook for her instead of doing it herself. By doing this, she appears to force the soldier to adopt the traditional role of the *soldadera*. Notwithstanding these actions, she too returns to tradition in many ways. She settles down, marries, and has a child with her first love. As they begin to return to more traditional ways, he threatens to abandon her when she bears him a mulatto son (or daughter in the film version) and would have done so were it not for Tita's proving to him — through her mother's secret letters — that their child is legitimate. So even the most non-traditional characters appear to return to some sense of tradition, once more emphasising the novel's conservative ideology.

However, it is significant to note that, though Gertrudis is the sister who is most radically different, it is not until she is physically carried off the ranch by a soldier, that she is able to change. Only once out of the territory of the 'tradition enforcer', Mamá Elena, does her character begin to take shape, a character which is quite different to that of her sisters.

Mexico/USA relations and malinchismo[2]

Both the novel and the film version of *Como agua* mention that Piedras Negras is the town in Mexico nearest to the De la Garza ranch. Thus the setting is a border town, though we hardly ever see it in the film — only a small glimpse in a background shot when Pedro and Tita are talking as young friends/*novios*, and a quick glimpse of Gertrudis and Chencha walking through it. Nevertheless the setting demands closer examination.

Throughout the narrative one thing remains clear: the United States of America is highly favoured in almost every way. The majority of supplies for the ranch are bought there. The De la Garza family goes to Eagle Pass when there are important things to be bought, such as supplies for the birth of Rosaura's baby. US medicine is seen as superior. Dr Brown is unable to attend Rosaura's labour (he was the doctor of choice), but when Rosaura's birth turns out to be particularly difficult, Mamá Elena specifically requests Dr Brown to come every day until she has recovered. We also learn in this episode that Dr Brown's medical relationship with the family is not a one-off, but is long-standing since, on this particular visit, he comments on how much Tita has grown since the last time he saw

---

[2] Referring directly to Hernán Cortés' concubine and translator, La Malinche, this term refers to a preference for all things foreign over and above what is produced nationally.

her. The USA is also where Tita is sent to recover from a mental crisis.

One example of the film's bias towards all things American is the De la Garza family's ability to speak English.[3] Though this is even more evident in the film than in the book (as we hear it from the characters themselves), we learn on various occasions that several members of Tita's family speak perfect English. It even becomes an object of comment when Dr Brown's aunt praises Tita, 'por el perfecto inglés que hablaba' (p.222). Mamá Elena explains that Pedro, the only male living in the De la Garza household, also speaks English perfectly and, for that reason, (and because of his accounting skills), he is able to live and work in San Antonio, Texas. It appears that the father, Juan De la Garza, socialises with English speakers as well, which would have been fairly normal for a Mexican of upper-class standing (*34*, pp.8–9). After the birth of Tita, he is seen celebrating with English-speaking acquaintances. Mamá Elena also has personal links to the USA as her secret lover was of American extraction.

Moreover it is the United States, rather than other regions of Mexico, that is chosen for different episodes of exile. When Mamá Elena suspects that Tita and Pedro are becoming too close, she sends him and Rosaura to San Antonio, Texas. As previously mentioned, Tita is sent to the USA when she has a mental breakdown. Dr Brown opts to take her to his home instead of to an asylum — ultimately a move which allows Tita to fully recover. Finally, it is Esperanza who takes the De la Garza family line on its final (and possibly permanent) step over the Rio Grande into the United States — the significance of this will be discussed in more detail below.

However, if *Como agua* favours the US, there are a few ways in which Mexico is shown as superior. Food is viewed as vastly superior in Mexico. Tita believes so (she finds no enjoyment in the food prepared by Caty at Dr Brown's house, but she is magically

---

[3] Margarita Hidalgo's study of the use of Spanish and English in the US-Mexican border demonstrates, with statistical proof, that the higher the socio-economic status of the family in Mexico, the more probable it is that they will have a good command of English (*37*, p.9).

cured by a plate of Mexican soup brought to her by Chencha) and Dr Brown also appears to favour Mexican food. Dr Brown's aunt, when presented with a simple dish of beans cooked by Tita, applauds her cooking and assures her that it is much better than what is normally found at the doctor's home in the US (p.222).

As portrayed in *Como agua*, there is a strong tendency for Mexican women to be preferred by American men. The author does not state the nationality of his first wife, but once Dr Brown becomes a widower, we see how he is drawn to Tita — the only woman who has been able to capture his heart since his wife's death, and perhaps the only woman who is able to remain in his heart. When Tita decides to decline Dr Brown's marriage offer, he never remarries. Alex also prefers to marry a Mexican (though she too was originally 'produced' in the US). Mexican women are portrayed as the desirable spouse, rather than a partner from the USA. In the Brown family marrying outside the Anglo-Saxon clan appears to be a family tradition, as Dr Brown's grandfather kidnapped a Kickapoo Indian woman and made her his wife. However, Alex's marriage to Esperanza is much more easily accepted than that of his great-grandfather. It is likely that this is a social comment on middle America's inability to accept the subaltern[4] from its own territory, i.e. American Indians.

Male Castration

One of the more violent scenes which takes place in *Como agua* is told to us by Gertrudis. While on assignment to find a mole within her troops, one of the best men from Gertrudis' battalion uses the help of several prostitutes. Once the spy has been found, a trap is sprung and he is captured. Then Gertrudis' soldier violently kills the traitor and cuts off his genitals. Since such brutality is uncharacteristic of the man, the *generala* asks him why he acted in this way. The soldier responds that, upon learning that the spy was

---

[4] In this guide, when not used in a military context, the word 'subaltern' is used to mean 'non-hegemonic' and 'marginalised'.

also the man who had raped a member of his family, he castrated him as a way of redeeming his family's honour.

Much earlier in the novel Tita tells us of another significant castration scene. Upon setting the date of Rosaura's wedding, twelve chickens are bought with the purpose of fattening them up for the wedding feast and, as they are all male they need to be castrated. Tita is punished for disobeying her mother earlier by being made to help with the preparations for the wedding feast, which include castrating the roosters. Finding that such an operation proves to be too much for her, making her physically ill, Mamá Elena challenges her:

> ¿Qué te pasa? ¿Por qué tiemblas, vamos a empezar con problemas? Tita levantó la vista y la miró. Tenía ganas de gritarle que sí, que había problemas, se había elegido mal al sujeto apropiado para capar, la adecuada era ella […] Mamá Elena, leyéndole la mirada, enfureció y le propinó a Tita una bofetada fenomenal que la hizo rodar por el suelo, junto con el pollo, que pereció por la mala operación. (pp.25–26)

Here one of Mamá Elena's roles is clearly suggested to be that of a castrator. If castration is viewed as 'to geld or emasculate', one of her victims is definitely Tita, who is deprived of marriage and motherhood by her mother's traditions. Metaphorically the matriarch castrates almost all of the male characters with whom she comes into contact.

In the case of her husband, Juan De la Garza, Mamá Elena cheats on him and, while ultimately she does stay with him, she emasculates him by having sexual relations with another man, and by raising doubts as to the parentage of the middle daughter Gertrudis. Her later lack of interest in men — and one might say her disdain for them — is made clear during a meal following her grandson's baptism. Commenting on her interest in sending the only male members of her family to Texas (her son-in-law and her only grandson), the priest (a logical advocate for family and marriage) advises her against it, reminding her of the unstable political climate

caused by the Mexican Revolution. She baulks at the priest's idea
that it is 'important to have a man around the house' and shows her
contempt for men both in the past and in the present:

> Nunca lo he necesitado (un hombre) para nada, sola he
> podido con el rancho y con mis hijas. Los hombres no
> son tan importantes para vivir padre — recalcó —. Ni la
> revolución es tan peligrosa como la pintan, ¡peor es el
> chile y el agua lejos! (p.82)

If we consider the Mexican Revolution to be a 'man's enterprise',
she is also making little of this as well. What is ironic from her
statement is that in sending her son-in-law away, she unwittingly
causes her only legitimate grandson's death (since his only source of
nourishment is Tita's breast milk) and indirectly contributes to her
own. This is because she is the only woman present when the bandits
attack the ranch, and the men are thus able to cause her injuries that
will directly contribute to her death.

Nonetheless, from the early stages of his relationship with her,
Mamá Elena effectively castrates her son-in-law. This happens in
several ways. Mamá Elena metaphorically castrates him by denying
him marriage to the woman she knows he loves, Tita, and instead
offers Rosaura's hand in marriage. In this way she puts him
constantly near the object of his desire, while at the same time
denying him access to it.

Despite criticism from the townsmen (as most appear to know
that Pedro and Tita have a special relationship), Mamá Elena has
Pedro move into her home, instead of letting him take his new wife to
his parents' home, which is much more common in Mexico and other
parts of Latin America. Although this is obviously beneficial to
Pedro and Tita, it nonetheless places Pedro where he will be subject
to further control and castration. Such control is obvious throughout
the text. For example, when Pedro gives Tita a bouquet of roses to
congratulate her on a year of being the ranch's cook, Mamá Elena,
merely with a look, orders him to go and apologise to his wife for
having given Tita roses (p.47).

While alive, and even after her death, Mamá Elena frustrates several of Pedro's attempts either to run away with Tita or to be intimate with her. For example, when Pedro and Tita watch Gertrudis run off with a soldier, Pedro is about to ask Tita to run away with him. However Mamá Elena interrupts him and frustrates his attempt. Similarly, when Pedro and Tita are about to become intimate outdoors on a summer's night, Mamá Elena cries out for Tita, causing both to retreat to their respective beds. Finally, Mamá Elena's ghost causes a lantern to explode and severely burn Pedro while he is serenading Tita outside: punishment for having disobeyed her will.

Even though it is true that Mamá Elena does effectively castrate Pedro — he is never able to give Tita a child — in some respects he is able to have the last laugh. In the end, Pedro participates in a sexual relationship with both Rosaura and Tita. He sires the only De la Garza child and, in a sense, is able to protect her from her mother's family tradition by allowing her to marry a man who removes her from Mexico and the ranch. While he may be a castrated patriarch, he has effectively helped to change the direction of future family tradition.

Doctors and Healing

One of the themes in *Como agua* is illness and ailments, be they spiritual (those battling with challenges such as depression or lack of attention) or physical (pre-eclampsia and serious burns). Sometimes medicine is used to treat other conditions that are not precisely ailments, but which do require medical care, such as pregnancy and childbirth. Each of these is treated in different ways, some with both traditional and modern medicine, others with either one or the other. However, those who help in the healing process can be placed into two categories: the modern and the traditional.

Most of the medical advice and attention given by women in *Como agua* is traditional. There are at least four women who take part in different healing processes on different occasions: Chencha, Luz del Amanecer, Nacha, and Tita.

Though her role as a healer may be brief, Chencha's help is crucial. After losing her mind upon hearing of her nephew's death, Tita falls into a deep depression which she is aware of, but from which she appears unable to escape. While Dr Brown takes care of her, and offers an appropriate physical environment which should be conducive to healing, ultimately it is Chencha and her belief that 'Los caldos pueden curar cualquier enfermedad, física o mental' (p.123) which allows Tita to return to a healthy state of mind. After bringing Tita a bowl of *caldo de colita de res* from the ranch, Chencha and Dr Brown witness its magical effects, which allow her to break her silence and to rejoin society.

While Tita is in Eagle Pass, recovering at Dr Brown's home, she experiences another magical healing episode, which allows her to 'meet' Dr Brown's grandmother, a Kickapoo Indian.[5] One day Tita smells the aroma of tea brewing and, following her nose to the location of the infusion, she encounters an indigenous woman who reminds her very much of her own mother figure, Nacha, and who silently offers her a cup of tea. Tita finds this drink comforting in that it seems both familiar and new at the same time, and it reminds her of the maternal influence she found in Mexico while with Nacha. When later commenting on this experience to Dr Brown, he calmly explains that Tita must have seen his grandmother's ghost. We learn that the Indian woman has dedicated her life to discovering the medicinal properties of plants — including the use of Tepezcohuite (*Mimosa tenuiflora*), a plant later used by Tita to heal Pedro's burns.[6] Though rejected by Dr Brown's family due to their 'North-Americanness' — an obvious reference to the cultural ignorance and hypocrisy initially

---

[5] In his study of the Kickapoo Indians in Mexico, Latorre notes that the Kickapoos made use of a large variety of plants for medicinal purposes. Some of these were from Mexico, others were imported (*41*, pp.237-38). While it is true that 'Kickapoos guard their medicinal practices with an extreme secretiveness' (*41*, p.237), it is almost certain that they would have known and made use of Tepezcohuite and other local herbal remedies as well.

[6] The documented use of this plant for medical purposes (e.g. burns) and its medicinal properties has existed for over 100 years (*32*, p.543); however it is believed that the folk use of this plant has been around for much longer.

found in the Brown family, as the indigenous grandmother is arguably more North American than any of them — she is accepted as the family doctor after she facilitates the miraculous recovery of her father-in-law, following a botched medical procedure. Though the only specific cure we are told about is the use of Tepezcohuite, the narrator informs us that Dr Brown was becoming more and more convinced that his grandmother's medicinal knowledge was superior to modern medicine. It is by referring to this same plant, which is often known as the 'skin plant' for its ability to help people heal without scars (*4*, p.100), that Esquivel is able not only to comment on folk medicine in Mexico, but also to draw attention to a case in which modern scientists have proved that this medicine is a cellular regenerator, an analgesic, and even a stimulant for hair growth (*4*, p.100). The narrative portrays Dr Brown as an early advocate of a medicine which, in our time, has proved to have specific medicinal properties. However, the folk medicines and methods are not only used to cure physical ailments, such as haemorrhages and damaged skin. They can also extend to the treatment of the spirit, such as the tea she gives Tita.

Nacha's influence is used in the healing of both the body and spirit. She uses food to try to help Tita overcome her sadness on learning that Pedro will marry Rosaura. Tita prays for Nacha's aid when she is required to help Rosaura give birth. After her prayer (as often happens with her cooking as well) she knows exactly what to do, and how to help her sister give birth and to take care of the baby, since Nacha has been whispering instructions in her ear. This whispering in her ear is repeated by Nacha's ghost when Pedro is burned by Mamá Elena. On this occasion we see the similarities in indigenous knowledge (both Dr Brown's grandmother and Nacha are aware of the curative properties of this plant) as well as the positive results of its successful application.

Finally, while Tita appears to bring about the biggest changes by the use of her culinary talents (something that will be discussed later pp. 41–53), she can also be seen as one who cures using traditional methods. She describes herself as someone who can identify with a healer/cook when she first comes into contact with

Luz del Amanecer (p.110). We have seen that she believes in the curative powers of different soups, but she also uses popular wisdom to cure ailments — often this involves food or food products (such as cocoa oil for her dry and chapped lips, or mashed raw potato and egg white to soothe a burn). However, in almost every case where she heals, at least part of the remedy she uses to cure broken bodies is dictated to her by her mentor/mother, Nacha.

If one were to read the narrative metaphorically, one could also see it as a metaphor for the broken body. The De la Garza family could be seen as crippled by their family tradition, which makes a servant of each youngest daughter. Tita could thus be seen as the family's healer, because it is she who puts in motion the actions which bring an end to the De la Garza tradition. She is the protagonist who breaks tradition by creating more awareness of the debilitating effects of the practice (mostly on the youngest daughter) and who then verbally fights it, finding allies such as Pedro, who help to ensure that the tradition is not enforced. So in different ways, these four women healers, Tita, Chencha, Luz del Amanecer and Nacha, successfully combat human ailments. Often they are physical ailments but they treat spiritual and mental ailments as well.

In contrast to the four women, Dr Brown represents modern medicine. He is the doctor whom the De la Garza family trusts with serious family ailments. Perhaps it is significant that it is usually Mamá Elena who calls on him to come to the family home (whether because she is the matriarch or because she trusts modern medicine is not made clear). Dr Brown uses modern methods. He carries out surgery to allow Rosaura to give birth to her second child. He also experiments in a modern laboratory. He uses the same one as his Kickapoo grandmother, but he has modernised its equipment and supplies. He also knows about modern ailments. For example, he is the only one able to describe Rosaura's sudden swelling during her first labour as a symptom of the pre-eclampsia from which she is suffering (as well as being able to treat it successfully). Though intrigued by, and initiated into, the curing arts by his Indian grandmother, Dr John Brown received formal medical training. These are the methods he uses when treating the De la Garza family (while it is assumed that he must have other patients, they are not mentioned). However, Dr Brown is open to other methods of healing, as well as having an interest in explaining human nature. While Tita is staying with him he explains to her his grandmother's rather fantastic theory that all of us have a box of matches inside of us, which can be lit by a loved one, and which allows us to experience intense emotions (but that lighting all of them at once can bring about death — even though the effect is beautiful) (p.116). The text portrays him as a man who is, after many years with modern medicine, returning to the beliefs held by his Indian grandmother. In this respect he is shown as progressive, since he dedicates a great deal of time to proving his grandmother's theories by use of scientific methods. So in this sense, *Como agua* looks at medicine from both a modern angle (allowing for some open-mindedness for other methods and ideas) and from a traditional/alternative stance. However, it depicts modern medicine as able to heal the body, but as not quite so successful with the mind. This notion is clearly seen when Dr Brown provides Tita with a safe environment, and tries to encourage conversation as a means of therapy, but Tita is only successfully cured when she eats the soup that Chencha has prepared for her. Thus, modern medicine is good for the body, but it is soup, *Como agua* seems to be suggesting, which soothes the soul.

Another aspect of alternative therapies that can be found in *Como agua* has to do with a somewhat puzzling ailment. When Pedro agrees to marry Rosaura, Tita begins to suffer an inexplicable emptiness and coldness in her soul. Obviously this is caused by Pedro's promise to Tita not being fulfilled in the way she had desired. This emptiness is repeatedly emphasised throughout the text. There are a few moments when a remedy appears to be applied, such as when Pedro shows his love towards her, as at her sister's wedding (p.36), and when he stops to admire Tita's breasts while she is cooking (p.67). Happiness for Tita (and the end of her inexplicable feeling of coldness), is finally achieved when Pedro asks her to marry him (p.237). In this case, though it is something of a cliché, Pedro can be seen as the person who offers spiritual healing to Tita and, in this respect, he too participates in some of the healing, though one could also argue that he is merely mending what he has broken, since it was his unfulfilled promise that appeared to cause Tita's ailment.

In many different ways *Como agua* is a novel about healing and medicine. This idea can be applied to both physical healing and to mental and spiritual healing. As we have mentioned, one could view the narrative as one which demonstrates to the reader how Tita is able to heal a crippling family tradition as well as herself. Physical ailments are treated and spiritual ailments are also considered. The coldness Tita feels as a result of the time she spends away from Pedro, and the lack of affection that he shows her, the mental collapse that she suffers from the loss of her nephew, and the isolation and abandonment she endures within her own home are all, in one way or another, grist to the novel's mill. In these different treatments Esquivel shows us different types of medicine and healing, namely traditional and modern. By using characters which represent each side of the healing debate, namely Tita and Dr Brown, Esquivel suggests how the old and the new are fused in the Mexico of the time.

There are several women who practise traditional medicine in *Como agua*, and it is used for several different purposes. Tita is the central character. She has two different methodologies and both are taught to her by women of indigenous extraction. One is the use of food. This can be for comfort — as when she uses food to recover memories and to fulfil a desire for nostalgia, or when she uses warm chicken eggs to try to warm the spiritual coldness from which she suffers. The other is more practical — the use of cocoa oil to keep her chapped lips from cracking, for example. Others are a little more esoteric, such as the use of soups to heal physical ailments (this is discussed in further detail below). Tita is portrayed as somewhat naive in certain aspects of traditional healing and medicine (even in preventative medicine such as birth control, which Gertrudis teaches her), but what allows her to continue in her role as a healer is both the fact that she is in tune with the voice of traditional healers, such as Chencha, Nacha and Luz del Amanecer, and that she is open to new ideas of healing — such as those she is taught by Doctor John Brown.

Luz del Amanecer is another example of this, having come from a Native American Indian tribe which relocated several times, from the northern United States to Texas and Coahuila, Mexico (*4*, pp.60–61). Nevertheless, Luz del Amanecer is a character about whom we know very little. For example, we do not know on which side of the border she lived prior to becoming part of Dr Brown's family. However, what is clear is that she brings a healing element to the novel. Having become familiar with the spirit's presence while Tita is at the doctor's home in Eagle Pass, when Pedro suffers a serious burn, Luz del Amanecer, through Nacha, shows Tita how to treat the burn with the special bark from the 'skin tree'. As with Rosaura's labour, the doctor congratulates Tita on a job well done. The man of modern medicine approves of Tita's work with traditional medicine and Tita can be viewed as a symbol of reconciliation between both approaches.

One of the major differences between these two healers is that Tita does not look for opportunities to heal and does not openly experiment with healing. Most of her work in this area arises because she finds herself in a situation where someone requires attention, and she is the person who is around to help. She does not wish to be involved in Rosaura's childbirth, but does lend her full aid when required.

Whilst traditional medicine is present throughout the story, preference is given to modern medicine. For example, after a serious incident, as with the birth of the first child (where traditional methods are used only because Dr Brown is prevented from attending by the disruptions of the Mexican Revolution — the second child was born under his care) and the serious burn sustained by Pedro, after traditional methods have been applied the doctor of modern medicine is always called to check that all is in order. Dr Brown speculates that Mamá Elena killed herself by taking an accidental overdose of a modern medicine, Ipecacuanha. Ironically, she is a staunch supporter of modern medicine (p.136). She insists that the doctor is called, and that he returns often, and even insists that Rosaura's family move to the USA to receive better medical care. Nonetheless, the modern aproach — represented by Dr Brown — still appears to accept the value of the traditional methods used by Amerindian healers.

Dr Brown, while he represents modern medicine, is also viewed as a radical thinker. Not only is he a medical practicioner, who consults, makes house calls, and seems to treat almost everyone and everything in the narrative — including Tita's mental crisis. He also conducts experiments and is regarded as a medical researcher. As the grandson of Luz del Amanecer, he is portrayed as a person who wishes to create an amalgam of what is good in both modern and traditional medicine. This is clearly shown in the episode in which Pedro is treated by Tita with the Tepezcohuite. Although this plant is a herbal remedy, and considered somewhat folksy in its origin, Dr Brown tells those around him that he believes in the remedy, which was taught to him by his grandmother, and that he wishes scientifically to prove to the modern medical community its great benefits.

Dr Brown between the past and the future in his laboratory

The desire of Dr Brown to blend both the traditional and the modern is illustrated in the film by a scene in which he is seen speaking with Tita in his laboratory, while making matches and explaining the process to her. Even the telling of the story is significant, because it shows the reader how Brandt, in the search for something quite mythical, the philosopher's stone,[7] found phosphorus, a key ingredient in the modern method of making fire — the match. While he is speaking with Tita, Dr Brown is making matches. In front of him (symbolising the future) is his modern scientific equipment which seems to suggest that the future is in science. Behind the doctor (making reference to the past and framing him), are artistically drawn pictures of roots and plants used in traditional medicine. Dr Brown is in the middle of this compositional frame. Whilst he is a modern doctor, he wishes to incorporate traditional methods into his work and to make them all one, just as he is the product of a family of traditional healers (e.g. Luz del Amanecer) and modern doctors. (It is in the telling of this story of the doctor's grandmother that we observe some of the past shortcomings of modern medicine and the wisdom of the traditional, as we are told of the man who was about to bleed to death in a blood-letting incident, who was then cured by the herbs applied by the Kickapoo Indian woman. This is a timely reminder not to underestimate the value of such knowledge.) The desire to combine both fields can also be seen in the fact that Dr Brown wants to create a union between himself and Tita, the modern and the traditional. In some ways it could be said that Dr Brown is both a product of (as a grandson) and a protector of (as a doctor) the social subaltern, as he defends not only his grandmother's work, but also that of others like Chencha and Tita. However, it would seem that, unlike his grandfather, his desire to mix with the subaltern was unfulfilled. Ultimately, Tita does not accept his invitation; however, she does, one might say, help prepare the way for the eventual mixing of the two societies as she prepares Esperanza to marry Alex. So, in the end, the two worlds of knowledge are seen to combine: the woman versed in the traditional arts, Esperanza, marries Alex who has been schooled by his modern father and who goes on to receive his further education at one of the most prestigious centres of learning in western society: Harvard University.

---

[7] The philosopher's stone is said to be 'a stone or substance thought by alchemists to be capable of transmuting base metals into gold' (*46*, p.893).

3. *Culinary elements in* Como agua

Food and Sex

As suggested in the epigraph, 'A la mesa y a la cama, sólo una vez se llama', *Como agua* is a narrative which strongly intertwines sex and food. Apart from provoking some of the more magical and entertaining moments within the story, the creation and consumption of food (and the consequences thereof) is a leitmotif that permeates the whole of the story.

In one of the flashbacks in *Como agua*, we see that it is during a special dinner that Tita first becomes aware of Pedro's gaze. (While this scene is clearly represented in the film as well, there is an even earlier flashback to Tina's youth, and the viewer sees how Pedro admires the child-Tita from a distance while she serves food at a dinner party.) The hot and burning sensation she feels from Pedro's gaze makes Tita feel as if she herself is a piece of *buñuelo* dough, being boiled in hot oil and being prepared to be consumed. It is on this occasion, with such clear symbolic connections between love and food, that the reader witnesses Pedro confessing and promising his undying love for Tita (p.15).

Though forbidden to marry, Tita later discovers that she and Pedro are able to communicate sexually through food. The best example of this telepathy, and one of the most celebrated scenes in the novel, occurs when the family eats Tita's quail in rose petal sauce. After Nacha's death, Tita becomes the head cook at the De la Garza ranch. To celebrate the anniversary of this appointment Pedro gives Tita a bouquet of pink roses. Rosaura runs away crying and offended, and Mamá Elena orders Pedro to apologise to his wife and Tita to throw away Pedro's gift of love. Tita embraces the bouquet of roses so hard that she bleeds, and they change to a dark red colour. Tita does not throw the roses away; but rather, prompted by Nacha's spirit, she creates a dish of roasted quail in a sauce made from the rose petals.

During the meal, magical events begin to occur. Rosaura takes three bites and leaves the table under the pretext of feeling ill. Mamá Elena complains that the food has too much salt. However, Pedro consumes every bite in a state of ecstasy, even to the point of exclaiming 'Este es un placer de los dioses' (p.50). Gertrudis, on the other hand, experiences a strong aphrodisiac effect:

> Parecía que el alimento que está ingiriendo producía en ella un efecto afrodisíaco pues empezó a sentir que un intenso calor le invadía las piernas. Un cosquilleo en el centro de su cuerpo no la dejaba estar correctamente sentada en su silla. (p.50)

She then begins to fantasise sexually about a *Villista* soldier whom she has seen earlier. During the meal Tita, in a metaphorical sense, becomes the food and is consumed by Pedro.

> Tal parecía que en un extraño fenómeno de alquimia su ser se había disuelto en la salsa de las rosas, en el cuerpo de las codornices, en el vino y en cada uno de los olores de la comida. De esta manera penetraba en el cuerpo de Pedro, voluptuosa, aromática, calurosa, completamente sensual. (p.51)

It may also be significant that, in their first sexual encounter, it is Tita who penetrates Pedro. He is the passive sexual element, allowing himself to be penetrated by the object of his love. Here we cannot help but notice the religious comparison between Christ and the sacrament, when the bread and wine become the body of Christ, which is then consumed by devout followers in order to enter into a special relationship with Him.

In this experience an unexpected love triangle is formed, which the narrator explains to the reader:

> Parecía que habían descubierto un código nuevo de
> comunicación en el que Tita era la emisora, Pedro el
> receptor y Gertrudis la afortunada en quien se sintetizaba
> esta singular relación sexual, a través de la comida.
> (p.51)

However, on this occasion, Gertrudis becomes the physical
embodiment of the sexual feelings of Pedro and Tita, becoming so
sexually energetic that she finds it necessary to work in a brothel in
order to satisfy her appetite. This will be the only time such a triangle
is formed, because almost immediately after the meal the middle
daughter leaves her family home for good. In this way, Tita's magical
food not only has significant amorous effects, but it serves as the
springboard for Gertrudis' independence from the family home.

Other sexual experiences are closely related to meals. It is after
having dinner that Pedro and Tita have their first physical, sexual
encounter (p.159). After Alex and Esperanza's wedding, for which
Tita caters, the *chiles en nogada* are served. This meal also has
aphrodisiac effects, causing everyone who eats some of the dish to
feel an immense desire to make love to their partner — and some do
so. One aspect which differentiates this final event from the others is
that, on this occasion, we see that Tita is able to recognise her sexual
feelings, caused by her cooking, and act on them (as opposed to
forming a part of a love triangle in which others would physically act
out her desires, or simply being the passive agent of Pedro's love, as
when he takes her virginity).

However food is not always related to sex in a positive way.
On various occasions it is implied that food actually prevents sexual
encounters. A prime example of this occurs during Pedro and
Rosaura's wedding. As mentioned above, while helping to prepare
Rosaura's wedding feast and cake, Tita cries into the cake batter.
This too appears to produce magical effects and, upon eating the
cake, everyone is overcome by feelings of 'nostalgia', 'melancolía y
frustración' and 'añora[nza] del amor de su vida' (pp.37–38)
followed by a vomiting spree which utterly ruins Rosaura's wedding
— the only one not affected by the cake being Tita (p.38). Such a

strange incident gives Pedro enough of an excuse to postpone the consummation of his and Rosaura's marriage for more than three months — when she finally finds the courage to tell him that she feels perfectly fine again.

One of the other ways in which Tita's cooking appears to prevent sex between Pedro and Rosaura is the physical effect it has on her. Even though Rosaura is not given meals specifically designed to make her gain weight, eating Tita's meals causes her to get very fat, and to suffer from chronic bad breath and revolting flatulence. Rosaura later confesses that this causes Pedro to cease sexual relations with her (p.171). This magical effect is something that occurrs only while she is living at the De la Garza ranch, since, when she goes to San Antonio, she magically loses weight while eating the same quantities of food.

In the end, not even Tita — who appears to be causing these effects without realising it — is able to cure Rosaura's food-related problems. Eventually, after a particularly bad bout of flatulence, they even cause her death. However, she is not the only person in the narrative to suffer death as a direct or indirect result of Tita's cooking. After an attack by bandits leaves Mamá Elena an invalid, Tita returns from her USA exile to care for her mother. Nonetheless, every time Mamá Elena eats a meal Tita has cooked for her, she perceives a bitter taste which she associates with poison (though nobody else who eats the food can taste anything amiss). Mamá Elena resorts to taking a strong emetic after eating, which causes a violent reaction and then her death (though in the film she is simply seen to have died after the men attack the ranch). Another sequence in which death is related to food occurs when Roberto, Tita's nephew, dies after being deprived of the breast milk Tita was feeding him when he moves with his parents to San Antonio. Though this could be interpreted as a death caused by Tita's secret; she only reveals to Pedro that she was breastfeeding the child in secret. Another example of the connection is when Nacha dies after a strong reaction to the wedding cake she and Tita make together. Finally, Tita and Pedro die as a result of their final lovemaking session, provoked by the *chiles en nogada* Tita makes for Alex and

Esperanza's wedding. Thus, the final meal combines food, sex and death as it closes the narrative. However it does so in such a way that the protagonists have a 'happy ending' — they are together at last in eternal bliss — as the narrator assures the reader that one should cook the recipes as a way of celebrating or immortalising Tita. So, while cooking does cause death, *Como agua* links this activity to immortality as well.

Food and the Calendar in Como agua

As would be expected from a book which describes itself as a cookery book, with a love story intertwined within its pages, *Como agua* uses food in many different ways with distinct results. However, it could be argued that, apart from sharing traditional Mexican recipes with the reader, two of its major functions are those of memory and magic. *Como agua* is divided into twelve different chapters, each one of which contains a recipe for a Mexican dish (with the exception of the month which teaches its reader how to make matches — which also play an important role in the story). Along with each recipe there is at least one link between magic and cooking. (Kari Salkjelsvik has pointed to this type of recipe narrative in *Como agua* as the writer likens the *Manual de Carreño* to a recipe book for women's life [21, p.171].) The next section will consider the connection between food and magic realism in the novel's monthly instalments.

If there is one magical place within the home it is the kitchen and, as it is food which creates most of the magical-realist episodes in the narrative, it is important to emphasise that the kitchen is the birthplace of this magic (something which will be further demonstrated in the chapter when Tita is not working in the De la Garza home). Tita is the main worker of magic — though she is not the only one. There are others too; for example Nacha and Chencha are also seen as having the gift of creating magical elements in their cooking. The kitchen is also the space where Tita is completely free to express herself. Indeed, though Mamá Elena does criticize her cooking at times, and treats her as her personal servant, she does not stop her from doing what she wants in the kitchen.

January

Magic is linked to cooking and Tita. As the narrative begins, we learn that the chopping of onions in the family kitchen, where Mamá Elena and Nacha are cooking, causes the unborn Tita to cry so much that her tears literally force her into the world; these then produce either five or twenty kilograms of salt when they dry on the kitchen floor (depending on whether you are reading the book or watching the film). This magical event equates Tita with being the salt of the earth — as that is what she has so abundantly produced with her birth — and not only suggests her noble personality, but also her role as the principal spice/flavour unit of the family. As salt takes an essential and central role in cooking, so Tita takes a central and essential role in the family and in the narrative.

February

February enlarges on the January idea about Tita's tears, and the influence that they will have on the month's events. Forced by her mother to help Nacha cook Rosaura's wedding feast and cake as a punishment for being disobedient, Tita eventually cries over the wedding cake's batter. Nacha's comments about this are significant: 'y ya deja de llorar, que me estás mojando el fondant y no va a servir, anda, ya vete' (p.34) she warns, as she tries some of the uncooked mixture herself. This turns out to be both true and false. Tita's crying over the batter causes it to produce magical effects at the wedding. Those who eat it become nostalgic and cry, and are then thrown into a vomiting frenzy. (Like a witch who is immune to her own magic, Tita is not affected by the wedding cake.) So in one way Nacha's words are prophetic; the cake is no good in that it has a terrible effect on those who eat it, but perhaps from Tita's perspective it is effective, because what is arguably the worst day of her life is also ruined for those who participate in it. Nacha, the only one who tries the cake in its uncooked form, is the one who is the most affected by it. She dies, apparently of nostalgia, and is found clutching an old photo of her true love.

March

The magical-realist episodes which are most memorable are those of February and March. This is no doubt because they contain some of the most dramatic magical sequences. Pedro gives Tita a bunch of roses as a gift, and with this she proceeds to make quail in rose sauce. Even the making of this dish is magical because, as Tita is about to throw out the roses, Nacha dictates the recipe into her ear and Tita proceeds to carry it out. Supposedly this is a pre-Hispanic dish, which further leaves the reader to speculate on its powers and abilities. The ingredients for this magical dish are suggestive in certain ways. Just as the name of the Aztec goddess of sexuality and fertility, Xochiquetzal,[8] means 'flower', the roses can be seen as sexually symbolic, and Pedro's giving them to Tita suggests that he desires to awaken her sexuality. Tita's serving them to him appears to suggest that she has decided to offer her sexuality to Pedro. Indeed, the fact that she returns the roses to him in a form that must be ingested, appears to indicate that she wishes to give herself to him and to become a part of him. The use of a non-domesticated creature — quail — also underlines the freeness of her spirit. These symbols take real form when Gertrudis and the rest of the family eat the meal. Tita, once again, is unaffected by it. Mamá Elena says the food is too salty — this could simply be a negative comment about the food, or it could suggest that — since the relationship between Tita and salt was established earlier in the book — there is simply too much 'essence of Tita' in the meal for her to enjoy it. Rosaura finds herself feeling ill, and excuses herself from the table. Perhaps she is just making a point, since her husband is obviously enjoying the meal and she does not want him to do so. Alternatively, it could be that one of the magical effects the food has on her is to exclude her from the love triangle by making her unwell.

Pedro, on the other hand, exclaims that the food is from the Gods and feels a voluptuous Tita enter him. True to the female/active-male/passive paradigm which is often found in the

---

[8] This goddess from Aztec mythology can be found in the sixteenth-century *Codex Ríos*.

narrative, by means of the roses she is the one penetrating him and
not vice-versa. The episode could be seen as the first time that Pedro
and Tita have sexual relations, albeit symbolically. At the same time,
Gertrudis becomes the synthesis of everything that is happening and,
whilst what Pedro may be feeling is internal, Gertrudis is full of
roses/sexuality and this begins to manifest itself externally. She
begins to feel hot and her sweat begins to take on a rosewater-like
quality; she appears to ooze female sexuality. She tries
unsuccessfully to cool herself by taking a cold shower (something
commonly related to the dampening of the male sexual appetite). She
runs out of the shower room, which her own 'heat' has ignited. Like a
bee to a flower, she runs straight to a man who has been bewitched
by her unique scent and they ride off together. There she exhausts
him sexually and — in an overtly magical-realist scenario — has to
work for a season in a brothel to satiate the enormous sexual desire
brought on by eating Tita's most famous dish. Once her whereabouts
is known, her past is symbolically erased by her mother, who throws
her pictures and birth certificate onto a burning fire and, like an
Egyptian pharaoh, prohibits anyone from mentioning her name. This
erasure by Mamá Elena is later reversed by Gertrudis herself,
through an act of cooking which will be mentioned later.

April

Here we are able to witness what could be considered two instances
of magic realism and food. When Roberto's wet-nurse is killed by a
stray bullet, it is Tita's desire for Roberto not to suffer hunger that
causes her to offer her breast. In doing so she produces milk for the
baby and is described as being 'Ceres — the goddess of food' (p.77),
mirroring other examples in literature. This experience, it could be
argued, allows her to experience a certain degree of motherhood, and
to be close to both Roberto and Pedro — possibly giving her more
happiness than ever before. This feeling is then transferred to the
meal of turkey in *mole* sauce that she makes for her nephew's
baptism feast. Even though her mother may have been angry with
Tita, she cannot help but notice that those who eat her *mole* enter into
a euphoric state, and have 'reacciones de alegría poco comunes'

(p.81). Just as Tita does not remember the Mexican Revolution, the death and chaos of which are all around, because she is so involved in her home life and the preparation of food, those around her also magically forget about the very real danger of life outside the confines of the De la Garza ranch.

May

The month continues with the magical-realist theme on food, cooking and the body. We find that in the summer months the family sleep together, but are separated by sheets which create tents. (In some ways this might be interpreted as a kind of failed harem. Pedro sleeps amongst a group of women in a hot desert-like climate, but it is a failure because the beauty he wants is out of his reach.) Pedro, lying awake at night, hears footsteps and recognizes them as Tita's, due to the 'fragancia peculiar que se esparció por el aire, entre jazmín y olores de cocina' (p.98). This leads to a brief encounter and a failed love attempt. Tita's special smell lends itself to the interpretation that at least some of the magic found in the kitchen, and her prowess at cooking is an element that is always with her. Tita has become a person with the ability to cook in ways which incorporate magic and, as suggested by the smell of jasmine, which are quite feminine too. In some ways the reader is reminded of of Remedios, la bella, from *Cien años de soledad*, who was rumoured to have a special and enchanting fragrance about her that captivated men (*34*, p.265). (Donna McMahon also makes comparisons between Esquivel's female protagonist and *Cien años de soledad* [*13*, p.19]). However, it is uncertain whether it is only Pedro who is able to detect this smell, or if it is a characteristic Tita possesses but which only Pedro ever mentions. It is also possible that this magical smell of cooking and flowers is a secret signal sent to her lover.

June

June is one of the exceptional months with regard to Tita, magic and cooking. There are no actual magical-realist episodes in the chapter, unless we wish to count Dr Brown explaining to Tita his ideas on internal phosphorus, the need to light the substance, and the need to stay away from people with 'cold breath', who can blow out our 'internal heat'. The warning is also against lighting our 'box of internal matches' all at once, because that would make a tunnel appear which would take us back to our divine origins. Here Dr Brown tells a magical story (which later comes true), proposing a scientific explanation for a magical-realist event. In the chapter we observe the contrast between science and magic. We are able to observe Dr Brown in his laboratory 'cooking', as it were, matches. It is in the scientist's kitchen that we are told the magical story which later is lived out by Pedro and Tita. The use of these matches becomes an important part of the final magical episode, when Tita eats the doctor's matches as part of her ritual to meet up with Pedro in the tunnel — a tunnel which Dr Brown has described, caused by too much ecstasy or interior fire. So, in a way, Dr Brown's cooking of the matches does have magical consequences — although it is Tita who puts the idea into practice. Notwithstanding this, there is no food in the chapter except for the bland North American food made by Caty and Tita does not cook at all. It is uncertain whether, had she cooked in the USA, she would have had magical experiences, but we do realise that the magic is caused by what she does in the kitchen, and when there is no magical cooking there is no magic.

July

Chencha's arrival further confirms that others too can cook with magical effects. When Chencha visits Tita, she arrives with a *caldo de res*. After just one spoonful of the *caldo*, Tita is miraculously cured of the mutism which Dr Brown has been trying to treat. Apart from expanding on the theme of magic and food, and the extension of these powers to other people, what is significant is Tita's reaction to having been healed by the soup:

> Los caldos pueden curar cualquier enfermedad física o mental, bueno al menos ésa era la creencia de Chencha y Tita, que por mucho tiempo no le había dado crédito

suficiente. Ahora no podía menos que aceptarla como
cierta. (p.123)

Here, for the first time, the reader sees that, while Tita does believe
that food is special, she is a little sceptical about some aspects of its
use. Her reaction suggests that perhaps she does not realise
everything that will happen when she cooks. Although there are some
occasions when she is quite sure of its results, there are others where
she is a little oblivious to the effect she has, as in the case of the
wedding cake where she seems slightly unaware, or even confused,
as to what has happened. The reader on the other hand, is encouraged
to put great faith in her magical role in the whole event. In reality,
Tita does understand that at least some of her food is special, and that
the form in which she creates things is important — this is of course
the reason why she tells Paquita Lobo to prepare food with lots of
love. Chapters June and July also show us that although when Tita
cooks, the magic does not seem to affect her, when others cook, as in
the cases of Dr Brown and Chencha, she can be affected magically
by what they make.

   Tita's lack of awareness of the magical effects of her food on
others can also be seen when she returns to the ranch. As she
reassumes her position after Chencha's rape and Mamá Elena's
injury, we see how Tita's cooking has a negative effect on Mamá
Elena. Everything she tries that Tita has cooked, tastes very bitter.
Tita is at a loss as to why this is happening, and others who try Tita's
food find it to have a pleasant flavour. The reader (the scenes are
omitted from the film version) is quite convinced that there is a
magical connection. However, Esquivel goes to even greater pains to
show us that it is Tita who is causing these side-effects, as we watch
how she cooks a meal and tries to pass it off as Chencha's. Perhaps
what we are experiencing here is not really a case of magic realism,
as traditionally defined, but simply magic, as Tita is surprised by the
results. Or perhaps she does realise what she is doing and there is
some cynicism here, though this hypothesis seems less plausible. The
fact that Tita has finally found the courage to stand up to her mother
seems significant, because it is only when she is unafraid of her

mother that her food acquires the ability to punish her. The bitterness seems to reflect her deep down bitterness towards her mother — later on she even says that she hates her.

August

The magic of Tita's cooking affects Rosaura as well. In this chapter we see how it has caused her sister to gain weight (a side effect which could either be attributed to Rosaura's wedding to Pedro, or to Tita becoming the ranch cook, as both events occur at the same time). As relations between Rosaura and Tita deteriorate, and as Tita feels particularly angry about Rosaura's decision to make Esperanza carry on the family tradition to be her mother's personal caretaker until she dies, we see that, apart from gaining weight, she also develops extremely bad breath and flatulence. Rosaura is determined to make Pedro love her, but Tita's cooking undermines all her efforts to make herself attractive to her husband, or to anyone else for that matter. If we have considered the idea that Tita cooks without any thought of the magical effects of her cooking, and if she doubts the magical effects of others' cooking (such as is the case with Chencha and her soups), it is in this chapter that she presents us with some ideas about her cooking which are definitely magical. When we read that the *champandongo* is not as good as usual, the narrator gives an interesting explanation:

> La comida no fue tan deleitosa … tal vez porque el mal humor acompañó a Tita mientras la preparaba… El champandongo es un platillo de un sabor tan refinado que ningún mal temperamento puede […] alterarse el gusto. (p.158)

This further reinforces the idea that, if when one makes things with love it can have special effects on the food, the opposite can be true as well. Whilst in some instances Tita appears to be unaware of, or disbelieving of, the relationship between magic and food, in others she accepts it as something quite normal, and even to be expected.

September

The month underlines the power of nostalgia with regard to food, and how it can magically invoke people and places. Mentally suffering from the thought that she might be pregnant after her encounter in the 'cuarto oscuro' with Pedro, Tita is making a *Rosca de Reyes* (even though it is normally eaten at Christmas) and hot chocolate for a special occasion. She spends a lot of time remembering just how much her sister Gertrudis liked to eat the sweet bread with a cup of hot chocolate when she was still living at home. Since she is beset by problems, Tita almost appears to be making her sister's favourite dish as if it were an invocation. She seems to want to make her return home, or at least to invoke her presence (as she has done with Nacha in the past) in order to have someone with whom she can share her problems, knowing that they will be understood. Tita's dish does, indeed, 'magically' conjure up her sister — Gertrudis stops her revolutionary fighting in order to go home and enjoy a party. So, on this occasion, the food becomes comfort food, in as much as it is able to bring Gertrudis home for a while, and to help Tita come to terms with her difficulties over the two men who love her. The chapter also continues to underline the ill effects Tita's food has on Rosaura — making her fat, giving her bad breath and flatulence. It also shows us how Tita appears not to realise that it is her cooking which is causing this in Rosaura, as she offers to prepare a special diet to counter these effects (without much success).

October

October sees Gertrudis cooking in the kitchen, as Tita has gone into the garden with Pedro to explain her suspected pregnancy to him. Though Tita is the one to begin making the *torrejas de natas* at the De la Garza ranch, Gertrudis agrees to finish them off when she realises how much her sister needs to talk to Pedro. It is important to analyse Gertrudis' work in the kitchen. Although we know that Gertrudis has worked in the kitchen before becoming a *generala*, she does not appear to be overly domestic. However she is so interested in the final outcome of the *torrejas* that she ignores Tita when her younger sister opens her heart. This could be due to the role food appears to play in Gertrudis' life — which is significant to the theme of food and magic. Just as Mamá Elena symbolically — and in some ways literally — eradicates Gertrudis' past when she runs off, by burning her birth certificate and her picture, Gertrudis appears, figuratively, or perhaps even magically, to recover her missing past in the De la Garza kitchen through the creation of her favourite food. However, using her authority as a *generala*, she calls on Sargento Treviño to help her in the making of the *torrejas*. At first, in what some have described as a comical representation (5, p.172), we see Treviño attempt to follow the recipe, but when she is afraid of his failure she comes to his aid as well. Here too, it takes both man and woman to form the final creation. In the end, the *torrejas de natas* are Gertrudis' 'niñez encerrada en un frasco' (p.203). If it is true that Gertrudis lost her childhood years in the family home because her mother erased them, she shows us how she is able to recover them by the making of a favourite food from her childhood. This depicts food as a kind of memory archive, magical in its restorative powers. It does not appear to be by accident that Gertrudis takes her childhood with her — perhaps to prevent its erasure once again, or simply to use it to withstand the trials of the Mexican Revolution.

November

Here we see how much Tita's food has been affecting Rosaura when, after a disagreeable encounter with Pedro and Tita, she locks herself in her room for a week and comes out having lost all of the weight that she put on while at the ranch. In this case, it is the absence of Tita's food which causes Rosaura magically to lose thirty kilograms in seven days. It is as if once Rosaura's suspicions are confirmed — that Tita and Pedro are in a not-so-clandestine relationship — that Tita's power over Rosaura's weight seems to disappear, though in the end she will still suffer from bad breath and flatulence. After the final confrontation, we see how Tita's knowledge of the magical power of emotion with regard to food ends up saving the dinner. Since Tita and Rosaura have been fighting while she is cooking a pot of beans, the beans will not finish cooking because they are 'angry'. So, in a magical-realist scene, we see Tita sing to the beans in order to calm their anger until they are cooked perfectly.

December

The final chapter contains two incidents relating to food and magic. It is in this section that we see how Rosaura's death magically occurs — brought on by a huge amount of flatulence that shakes the house, makes the lights flutter and causes Pedro to think that someone is having car trouble with an old Model T. Likewise, the section features another wedding for which Tita caters (helped by several anonymous hands, which are seen working on the meal). In this case the clock has jumped forward about two decades and it is now Esperanza who is getting married, the occasion being the counterpart to her mother's wedding. This time we see how the dish *chiles en nogada* causes a sexual uproar amongst the guests at the ranch. Instead of the guests feeling immensely sad and nostalgic, and then vomiting (as at Rosaura's wedding), the dish (which here is the main course rather than the dessert) causes them to become giddy and then, overtaken by sexual desire, to run off to fulfil their sudden urges. It is significant that the only character who goes off alone is Dr Brown (as even the priest and the local widow Paquita Lobo go off together), further emphasising that the love of his life is Tita, who is already taken by Pedro. It is once the guests have departed that Tita and Pedro leave to live out the effects of their food, and that is what causes the mythical destruction of the De la Garza ranch (not unlike the final destruction of the Buendía home in *Cien años de soledad* [*34*, pp.470–71]).

Food as an archive

In many ways food serves as an archive in *Como agua*. The scene previously mentioned, in which Gertrudis carries away her childhood in the form of a jar of *torrejas de natas*, is not the only example of this. For the protagonist, Tita, it is food which triggers many of the memories we encounter in the story. Apricots remind her of how she felt the first time Pedro saw her bare legs, the smell of *tamales* and

atole bring back fond memories of her mother figure Nacha, a
chorizo in her hands conjures up moments of the first time she
touched Pedro's body, and the smell of bean broth reminds her of
precious moments she has spent with her niece Esperanza. During
these and other moments, Esquivel comments on the power of food
to capture incidents in our lives — both good and bad — and to
bring them back at a moment's notice, without any effort on our part.
It becomes a catalyst for story-telling and, in this story/cookery book,
the means of telling a story.

Food brings pleasure and, like the *torta de Navidad* that Nacha
brings Tita on learning the terrible news of her sister's wedding, it is
used to comfort others. It also causes pain — such as the bitter taste
of the food Tita prepares for her mother. Food found in the novel
rarely takes the middle road, and even invokes visits from beyond the
grave. For example, the occasion when Nacha strokes Tita's head
while she is eating Chencha's *caldo de res*, or transforming the
cuarto oscuro into a *cuarto iluminado* just as Tita and Pedro are
about to enjoy the effects of the *chiles en nogada*, or at times
appearing simply to tell her how to cook a pleasing meal.

Food is used as a metaphor and, in a very real sense, it
becomes a part of the language of the text. Chencha complains about
Mamá Elena's mixing and matching, while arranging Rosaura's
wedding, by saying that you cannot switch future brides as if they
were a plate of *tacos* and *enchiladas* (p.12). It compares the
permanence of sexual experience when Pedro gazes longingly at
Tita's breast, with that of a piece of dough when transformed into
cooked tortilla. Once it has changed, from virginal to voluptuousness,
or from dough to tortilla, it can never return to its original form. Tita
uses food to mirror situations in her own life, such as when she
compares her thought-to-be pregnant body to a sprouting grain or
bean, which expands in order to give way to new life. Of course,
there is also the title of the book itself, *Como agua para chocolate*.
The phrase refers to the fact that, in Mexico, water is often used for
making hot chocolate, and when the water is ready for the chocolate

it is boiling.[9] This image of boiling water is one of heat, which in Mexican Spanish can mean that someone is angry: they have reached their boiling point. Another reading of it could refer to someone being hot as *caliente* or sexually aroused. If there is anger in the book on Tita's behalf (because there is no mistaking Mamá Elena's anger with the world and others — perhaps due to her forced marriage), it is more of a passive-aggressive anger, seen in the ill-effects her food has on her oppressors: Mamá Elena and Rosaura. She does not demonstrate an overtly aggressive anger, not even when confronted by her sister or by Pedro. What she does give in to is passion, and there are scenes in which an individual is *caliente* in many different ways and on many different occasions. Rosaura desires her husband (though he does not reciprocate the feelings). Mamá Elena desires her mulatto lover, Paquita Lobo desires the local priest, Gertrudis desires the revolutionary soldier who carries her off, and of course Pedro and Tita desire each other. Love and sex, illicit or not, are everywhere in the narrative and often the most passionate relationships are those which the famous *Manual de Carreño*, and society's rules, most often forbid.

Tita and Rosaura

There are some fundamental differences between Rosaura and Tita in their respective views of sex and they help to establish each person's distinct function within the love triangle. Though early on in the novel and film we witness Pedro's intentions with regard to Rosaura — that he is only with her in order to be near Tita — the fact that this really is his intention is made clear once they are married. Using the pretext that they should wait until they feel better, after suffering such strange effects when eating their wedding cake, Pedro waits about three months after the marriage until — at his wife's insistence — he takes the decision to consummate it. Both the book and the film take special pains to show the ritualistic manner in which this is

---

[9] 'Está como agua para chocolate' is defined by Shirley L. Arora as 'angry i.e... heated as is the water with which the chocolate drink is prepared'. One other exception to this definition, Arora notes, is when it specifies a pretty young woman as being 'ready, ripe' (*29*, p.43).

done. Sex is de-eroticised and given highly religious overtones. For example we see that the *sábana nupcial* is used when the husband and wife make love. While no real historical information appears to exist as to how generalised this use of the silk sheet was in pre-Revolutionary Mexico (its acquisition from a travelling merchant is one of the few moments when the Mexican Revolution is actually mentioned in the novel), it could be viewed as an instrument whose purpose is to de-eroticise sex because it prevents intimate contact between the man and woman, thus reducing sex to a mechanical act merely to create children. Pedro finally agrees to engage in sexual relations with his wife when he realises that he can no longer postpone his 'labor de semental' (p.39). He drives the point home when we see him praying by his bedside before performing his labour, and promising in his prayer that 'no es por vicio, ni fornicio, sino por dar un hijo a tu servicio' (p.39). He seems to be excusing sex with his wife Rosaura on the pretext that it is to have a child to raise in the holy faith.

When comparing Pedro's marriage to his relationship with Tita we see a completely different character. Though he has been described by Tita as someone without a large sexual appetite, what is clear is that he does desire sex with her. The idea of being with Tita is sexually exciting for him and, while he begins as a man of high moral standards, with the passing of time he begins to engage in much more risqué behaviour. For example, in the first years of his marriage to Rosaura, Pedro discovers his true love's body quite by accident. It is significant that Pedro's love for Tita exists even before he has a complete knowledge of her body — a romantic notion of love. While she carries fruit in her skirt, Pedro catches sight of her legs. Later, while grinding corn, he catches a glimpse of her breasts. Here, we note, he has begun to ogle Tita's body. He has gone from a person who has caught an accidental glimpse, to one who looks at Tita's breasts and changes them from 'castos a voluptuosos' (p.67) just by admiring them. It is also implied that Pedro's role as a voyeur has changed Tita in some way. Indeed, this experience is actually the fulfilment of a secret desire, which he has maintained since he saw Gertrudis' breasts bounce up and down while she was running away naked from the De la Garza ranch. Pedro later fulfills his desire to make love to Tita, to prevent her from leaving the ranch to marry Dr Brown. However, the relations they engage in within the 'dark room' are quite different from those that he has with his wife. Tita offers little resistance and the sparks literally fly from the shed where they make passionate love. There are no prayers or excuses for fulfilling their desires and passions on this occasion, or on any other occasion when they have sex. As the story proceeds, Pedro becomes more voyeuristic in his desires, and more sexualised as a character. We find him spying on Tita in the shower — annoying her by doing so. This coincides with a time when Pedro is completely uninterested in his spouse. He has fulfilled his duty as a husband and appears to see himself as free to explore his true sexual identity.

Once Pedro and Rosaura marry, Tita's life takes on a resonance similar to that of Penelope in Greek mythology.[10] On the wedding night, to stop the terrible cold which she feels inside, Tita begins to knit a blanket (p.18). In a magical-realist episode we watch her knit through the night —apparently not needing sleep — and finish it by the morning. While she says that she knits to protect herself from the cold, it could also be interpreted as an allusion to Penelope's strategem. She continues to knit through each night, going through any kind of wool she can find and creating a strange patchwork pattern, which grows as she waits for her lover. It is as if Pedro's time with Rosaura could be seen as the battle he has to fight in order to return to Tita. Indeed, it could be seen as a rewriting of one of the female archetypes that Tina Escaja describes in her critical essay (*2*, p.574). Likewise, one could read *Como agua* as a modern, Mexican version of the Old Testament story of Jacob, who is tricked out of marrying the woman he loves, Rachel, by being made to marry Rachel's sister, Leah. Esquivel's version is more tragic however, as the man is never offered marriage to the other sister. Tita's

---

[10] Penelope was the wife of Odysseus. She went to Ithaca to wait for Odysseus, while he had gone to war. Believing her husband was dead, other suitors pressed Penelope to marry them. She was faithful to her husband and postponed remarriage by weaving (and secretly unpicking) a shroud for her father-in-law for three years until Odysseus returned (*48*, p.460).

compulsion to knit while she waits for Pedro to return is not assuaged by his making love to her, or even by Rosaura's death. A more likely explanation is that the knitting helps to deal with the 'ansia y sufrimiento' that she feels when she is near Pedro (p.132). Surely this is anxiety and suffering, caused passively rather than actively, because although he is near they are still unable fully to express their relationship. This Penelope-like desire appears to end only when Pedro is fully hers, and no longer has obligations to Rosaura or Esperanza. However, on Pedro's return to Tita, we see how she creates what seems to be the wick that serves to light the apocalyptic fire which destroys the De la Garza ranch. Perhaps this is the reason why Tita's knitting expands to mythical/magical proportions as each night passes, while her magical ability to go through life without sleep, allowing her to perform such a feat, also adds to the magical-realist element. Alternatively, it could also be read as an allusion to the weaving of the fate of the De la Garza family and ranch, as Greek mythology itself might suggest.

Violence and the De la Garza Ranch

Violence is an important motif in *Como agua*. Whilst the narrative is full of repression and forced servitude, there is relatively little physical violence (though it is suggested that some violence, relating to the Mexican Revolution, is happening outside the ranch). The violence which occurs on the De la Garza ranch is almost always between women, and is mostly inflicted by Mamá Elena on Tita. Such punishment, handed out by her mother, makes her live in fear even after her mother's death:

> Tita físicamente tampoco tenía a su madre, pero aún no podía quitarse de encima la sensación de que le caería de un momento a otro un fenomenal castigo del más allá, auspiciado por Mamá Elena. (p.199)

Her fear is clearly the product of many years of punishment, both physical and mental. Whilst Mamá Elena is quick to throw things around, and to hit or slap her youngest daughter, the final straw appears to be when she breaks her daughter's nose, when Tita talks back to her on finding out that Roberto has died. It seems to be violence which pushes Tita to the edge of sanity and drives her from the ranch, only for her to return as the triumphant victim of her mother's abuse.

However, Mamá Elena's violence is not limited to Tita. When she realises that she is no longer able to control her daughter, she makes one last-ditch effort to destroy the relationship between Tita and Pedro. Although already dead, she returns and causes a petrol-lamp to explode on Pedro, causing him to receive serious — though not long-lasting — burns. If Mamá Elena is violent towards Tita, Rosaura is only verbally aggressive. In an incident studied elsewhere in this book (pp. 77–78), we see how they have a verbal showdown which ends in a strange magical-realist incident, but this appears to be the extent of the conflict between Tita and Rosaura. So, if Rosaura is to be viewed as a continuation of the repressive and violent Mamá Elena, she never goes to the same extremes as her mother.

Pedro and Dr Brown, however, turn the stereotype of violence on its head. While they see each other as rivals, there is never a real confrontation between the two men. Pedro never directly confronts Dr Brown, and even agrees that he and Tita should be married. However, he does not like this. He is seen as sulking, and is accused of acting like a 'chiquito emberrinchado' (p.211). Dr Brown, true to his image of a perfect gentleman, never threatens anyone — or even shows ill will for that matter. When his intuition tells him that Pedro is his rival, he tells Tita that he is willing to back down if she prefers Pedro to himself. This he does, and the text appears to suggest that this highly eligible bachelor then becomes a kind of old maid, patiently waiting for Tita's love. So, not only are these men non-violent, they are also *anti-machista.*

The only real act of violence which occurs on the ranch is when a group of bandits attack. Who these men are, and their exact intentions on the ranch, are not made clear. What we do know is that they arrive on the ranch unexpectedly, violently rape Chencha and attempt to do the same to Mamá Elena — she however, escapes rape but sustains an injury which leaves her paralysed from the waist

down, and ultimately leads to her proverbial fall from power and to
her death. Neither in the novel nor in the film do the outlaws speak,
but in the film version it is suggested that these men are from the US
side of the border. This can be inferred from the fact that, upon
seeing the men, one of the hired hands with Chencha yells in English,
'What do you want here?'. Their only response is to knock them
around before raping Chencha. It is uncertain why the bandits are
portrayed as Americans in the film version, or what they are doing on
the ranch in the first place. Perhaps their presence is simply an
excuse for a random negative event, thereby transferring blame from
the Mexican Revolution and Mexican men in general. Just as it is an
American who takes Tita away from the ranch (Dr Brown) — at
Mamá Elena's request of course — it is a group of Americans that
causes her return. However, perhaps it is simply to continue with the
non-violent depictions of the Mexicans who appear in *Como agua* (in
this case, the Americans are the violent ones). Possibly it is even a
subtle social comment from the present day, which is woven into a
story which takes place in the past, a comment on the idea that many
of the unexplained rapes and murders which take place on the
Mexican side of the border are caused by Americans who live on the
margins of the law.[11] The fact that their attack is apparently random,
and that they are never caught, might appear to support this idea.

   Whilst there are many passing references to revolutionary
violence outside the ranch, these are played down. One of the more
famous lines which deals with this theme is when Mamá Elena makes
light of the Revolution, seeing it as something which has been too
glorified, and claiming that eating hot chilli peppers — something
nearly universal in Mexican culture — without a glass of water
nearby, is worse:

> Ni la revolución es tan peligrosa como la pintan. Peor es
> el chile y el agua lejos. (p.82)

---

[11] Adam Jones offers a good overview of this type of crime perpetrated on
the Mexican border in his article 'Los muertos de Ciudad Juárez' (*38*, p.36).

Basically she laughs in the face of danger and, in the film, is joined by those around her, who seem to agree with her, at least outwardly. The narrative would have us believe that this is true. Later a supposedly tough general backs down when facing Mamá Elena — and even suggests that she too should fight in the revolution. The only violent act we see associated with the event itself (the rest is rumoured violence, or supposed violence and supposed collateral damage — as when Roberto's wet-nurse is hit by a stray bullet [p.76]) is the honour killing by one of Gertrudis' best soldiers. But this could be seen as an isolated incident, as both before and after the event he is portrayed as a perfect gentleman, and even as a man adored by women.

Rewriting History

Como agua can be viewed as a rewriting of history in several different ways. It is history written from the perspective of northern Mexico. In such a centralised country it is significant that this Mexican narrative is taking place on the Mexico/US border (though in real life the author is from, and lives in, the Mexican capital). We are looking at the Mexican Revolution from the point of view of those living on the northern border and in some ways we are able to see how this northern Mexican community is quite isolated from its country's centre (apart from the Chinese merchant who deals in contraband goods, no real contact is mentioned). This is also demonstrated by the heavy reliance on the US for supplies and technology. *Como agua*'s view of Pancho Villa's Mexico offers an alternative view of events that are occurring in the country in the early twentieth century.

History is also portrayed as written by women. As a cookery book, designed by women for women, we read about their lives as well. (Valdés discusses the idea that *Como agua* is meant to be a parody of the official cookery books existing at that time [25, p.79]). If not a feminist narrative, the novel does have a feminist feel to it. Women, not men, are the ones who make the major decisions, and who wield the power within the De la Garza ranch. However the reader can see a female-managed institution which mainly dominates

other females. In some ways, we are able to observe that the wielding
and abuse of power by Mamá Elena does not appear to differ from
that of other tyrants of the day, and Mamá Elena could be seen as
simply another Pancho Villa; nonetheless, the depiction of a woman
with these qualities does offer the reader an alternative reading of the
period.

The story not only includes women, it includes subaltern
women as well. It could be argued that they are the women who are
endowed with the most redeeming qualities. Luz del Amanecer,
Chencha, Nacha (all described by Román Odio as Tita's guides [20,
p.43]) — and, of course, Nacha's disciple, Tita — are portrayed as
subalterns with a wealth of knowledge. In particular, the alternative
subaltern matriarchs, Nacha and Luz del Amanecer, are renowned for
their knowledge, which at times is magical (for example, the recipes
given to Tita by Nacha) or superior to mainstream medicine (the use
of Tepezcohuite). Some may view it as belittling these subjects, since
Nacha and Chencha are also depicted as less refined. This can be
demonstrated by the way in which they speak. Their speech is
portrayed as crude, in the sense that it is obvious that they have not
been formally educated — though they are not portrayed as having
low intelligence, quite the reverse in fact, and in some situations they
are depicted as more sensible than others. A good example is
Chencha's comments on the absence of logic in Mamá Elena's
thinking — she offers to swap Tita for Rosaura when Pedro asks for
Tita's hand in marriage:

> ¿Ay sí, no? ¡Su 'amá habla d'estar preparada para el
> matrimoño, como si juera un plato de enchiladas! ¡Y ni
> ansina, porque pos no es lo mismo que lo mesmo! ¡Uno
> no puede cambiar unos tacos por unas enchiladas así
> como así!' (p.13)

Though Chencha expresses herself in a popular vernacular, her
reaction clearly mirrors that of the ordinary reader. However,
portraying them as speaking 'as they would' lends itself to a less
edited depiction of these characters. This is something lost in the

English translation (Britt's article offers additional information on the elements 'lost in translation' with regard to *Como agua* [*1*, pp.13–14]). The inclusion of the subaltern in this Mexican story allows many social strata to be displayed, and also shows the different ways in which they interact, thus allowing *Como agua* to integrate competing ideological views of Mexico's history and the evolution of its social classes.

Breaking Away From Tradition and Convention

In her article 'On Recipes, Reading, and Revolution', Kristine Ibsen argues that *Como agua* is a denouncement of the *Manual de Carreño* (*6*, pp.137–138) and, in the novel, *El manual de Carreño* is mentioned several times. It was written and published in the mid-1800s by the Venezuelan author Manuel Antonio Carreño. While the characters do not go into great detail as to its contents, on several occasions it becomes evident that Mamá Elena's daughters received instruction from it and were taught to follow its societal rules and rituals. However, most of the references come from Tita, when she complains that the manual's rules are too restrictive and impractical. Essentially, Tita cocks a snook at society when she underlines the failings of the book, and the ways in which the imprinting of its teachings on her mind have either prevented her from doing what she wants, or from carrying out one of life's essential tasks. This is evident as she describes the birth of her nephew Roberto:

> En las horas que pasó al lado de su hermana aprendió más que en todos los años de estudio en la escuela del pueblo. Renegó como nunca de sus maestros y de su mamá por no haberle dicho en ninguna ocasión lo que tenía que hacer en un parto. De qué le servía en ese momento saber los nombres de los planetas y el manual de Carreño de pe a pa si su hermana estaba a punto de morir y ella no podía ayudarla. (p.72)

As it is, Tita eventually begins to pray to Nacha for help. With the aid of her guardian angel she is able to deliver the baby successfully.

The whole episode appears to emphasise the important role of the subaltern in the novel. It is the traditional knowledge of the illiterate cook, Nacha — the popular archive — that empowers Tita to help her sister give birth. The conventions of society, school teachers, etiquette manuals, and even her mother, supply only protocol or knowledge, which in a time of crisis is not very useful. It is not the institution (library, family, or school) that appears to impart the required knowledge, but rather popular knowledge, or intuition. In this sense, *Como agua* could be seen as an anti-establishment text.

The use of the subaltern as a source of important information is not the only way in which alternative world interpretations, or counter-institutional ideologies, are presented. Some of them are quite simple, such as Gertrudis explaining a simple douching method to Tita, which she can use to avoid becoming pregnant. This sisterly tip points to several things. Firstly, that it is merely a piece of common knowledge used by the *soldaderas*, a popular solution to help one along in life, which Gertrudis has learnt from them. Secondly, Gertrudis, as a soldier and as a woman, is offering subversive religious advice to her sister. Tita, who by previous example and conversation is submissive and passive in her sexual relations, is being taught, by her sister — the most rebellious of the three —to be more proactive. It would appear that her time spent away from the De la Garza ranch provided Gertrudis with additional educational opportunities.

One other example of counter-institutional ideology in *Como agua* is the use of Freemasonry images. Although they are not mentioned in the novel, the film contains two subtle examples of the influence of Freemasonry. The first occurs a few seconds after Juan de la Garza suffers a heart attack while conversing with his friends. Immediately afterwards, we see what appears to be one of the Freemasons blowing out a candle. The cameras then focus on the mourners giving their condolences to Mamá Elena and her family. Then, quite briefly, they take the point of view of an unknown girl, who is looking through the partially frosted glass of a door behind which five Freemasons — dressed in their religious attire —

A furtive viewing of Juan de la Garza's funerary rites

carrying out a form of funeral rite for Juan De la Garza. No
explanation is offered, either by the the narrator or by the family. The
spectator is distanced from the scene, and is allowed to contemplate
it only briefly, from behind closed doors. The only view from within
the room, where the funeral rites are taking place, shows the young
girl peering through the glass. Only one of the girl's eyes is able to
see through the glass clearly (the frosted part blurs the vision of the
other eye). The cinematography is used as if to suggest: 'You see, but
not fully, nor clearly'. Thus we see that Juan, while he may have been
a Catholic, being also a Freemason he would not have prohibited it.
In death he was more strongly affiliated to this alternative religious
group than to the Catholic mainstream. This is especially significant
if one considers religion to be one of the more intimate links to one's
inner self.

Other Freemasonry imagery found in the cinematic version
relates to Dr Brown's explanation of everyone's inner-flame and will
be mentioned later. When Dr Brown opens his notebook, to explain
to Tita what happens when someone lights all of their 'internal
matches' at once, there are signs and symbols in the notebook that
suggest that they too are linked to Freemasonry. Perhaps the purpose
of all of this subtle symbolism is to suggest that the elite of the region

Freemasonry symbols in Dr Brown's notebook

(on both sides of the border) are involved with Freemasonry. This would make sense, because it is logical that the doctor would also form part of the local elite and thus participate in the organisation. (This is another link to the *malinchista* aspect of the narrative.) This elite family is obviously linked to the Freemasons, a group more associated with Great Britain or Protestant North America than with the Catholics in Mexico, whose elites might be closer to other organizations. The series of symbolic visual cues points to secret societies and elite religious groups, whose members possess an element of control over the workings of the local area, and since they are not mentioned in the novel, they suggest how the film offers, in places, an original interpretation of the novel.

4. An Alternative Reading of Como agua's Finale

Como agua is often seen as a celebration of Mexico and Mexicanness (*3*, pp.92–93; *9*, p.61; *20*, pp.41–42; *22*, pp.30–31), and in many ways it is just that. Food is central to the narrative, especially food linked to customs and celebrations — Christmas, weddings, baptisms etc. It is also the story of several generations of a Mexican family (though whether it is a typical family or not is widely disputed). *Como agua* also makes mention of, and contains, significant characters from various levels of Mexican society. It is possible to see the church (the priest), the poor (servants, Chencha, Nacha), the local busybody (Paquita Lobo), the local elite (the De la Garza family), the merchant class (the Chinese vendor who travels around Mexico), and even soldiers (Sergeant Treviño) from the time of the Mexican Revolution. This is not to mention numerous foreigners, who are seen in both the film and the novel, and who appear to be friends and confidants of the family, such as Dr Brown. However, while the book does celebrate Mexico, its people and its society, it can also be seen as the story of a family's departure from Mexico.

In one way it tells of the literal disappearance of the De la Garza family. Since Juan de la Garza only fathers two girls (Gertrudis is really a mulatto's daughter), and they appear to have no other family in Mexico (there is a brief mention of a cousin in Texas, though no specific family relationship is mentioned), the De la Garza family name disappears. This is because there are only girls in the family, one of whom never marries (Tita) and the only other living relative is Esperanza, who marries Alex Brown and who presumably makes her transition 'al otro lado' when she marries.

As alluded to in the *malinchismo* section, from the beginning of both the novel and the film we see that the De la Garza family is well-connected in the USA. When Juan celebrates the birth of Tita, he does so with his English-speaking friends, and Spanish is only used to deliver the bad news that Gertrudis is not really his daughter. The film also subtly underlines his association with the Freemasons (whose presence is more extensive in the USA than in Mexico) at the time of his funeral. As time passes, we become aware that all important shopping is done on the other side of the border. Important issues such as health are dealt with in the USA. When problems occur, the Mexicans tend to look to the USA for solutions. An example is when Mamá Elena suspects that there is a romantic affair between Tita and Pedro — the solution is to send her across the border to live with a cousin.

The family's departure from Mexico is simply portrayed. Of the two natural daughters of the De la Garza family, only Rosaura is married. (Interestingly enough Gertrudis is symbolically cut off from the family when she runs away — her birth certificate is burned, as are her photos. One could argue that since the birth certificate does not contain the name of Gertrudis' real father it is in any case inaccurate). Rosaura produces only one living child (though ironically the only boy she produces dies when he is taken across the border to live — perhaps symbolically foreshadowing the fact that the De la Garza name will end in the USA). The only remaining De la Garza grandchild child is Esperanza. It would appear that the idea, indicated by Esperanza's name, is that she will escape the oppressive traditions of her home town and live freely in the United States of America. Esperanza also becomes the hope for societal normality. If she is married to the man she loves, then she will be his legitimate wife and lover — this is also, indeed, the unfulfilled desire of both Rosaura and Tita.

Esperanza's future in the USA is alluded to at the time of her birth, when Dr Brown's son says he wants to marry the little girl (although Rosaura tells him that it will be impossible because of the family tradition). Tita and Pedro do everything in their power to prepare Esperanza for life in the north; they send her to school and make sure that she is able to communicate in English. Fortunately for her, her mother Rosaura dies (thus in effect liberating Esperanza), and there is no more opposition to Esperanza's relationship with, and subsequent marriage to, Alex Brown. We know little about this relationship except that it develops in a similar fashion to Tita's and Pedro's (both women feel as if they are burning inside with love when looked at by their soulmate). However what we do know is that after the wedding Esperanza leaves Mexico and travels north to live in Cambridge, Massachusetts while her Alex attends Harvard University.

In both the film and the novel, the reactions of those around Esperanza and Alex to their union, and to their departure from Mexico, are noteworthy. Everyone approves of the union as it is agreed that Esperanza could not have found a better partner in the whole region (p.241). When Pedro makes the sad announcement that they will be leaving to study at Harvard, the crowd's reaction is approving. The couple's hope of returning to the ranch also disappears when, on their wedding night, it goes up in flames as a result of the death of Pedro and Tita. Later, the family decides to build a small apartment complex on the property — where Alex will eventually live after Esperanza passes away (the home of their daughter is kept ambiguous in the novel, but we know that it is not located at the ranch). Alex's later residence at the apartment-building on the ranch alludes to the fact that, in the present day, many Americans go to Mexico to live out their retirement.

It is difficult to pinpoint exactly who provides the driving force for the family to leave Mexico. It is true that it could simply be the result of following true love — a natural result of a Mexican woman falling in love with an American man. However, given the family's, and the community's, relationship with the USA it could also be viewed as the best way to be upwardly mobile in a border community. Likewise, the US could simply be seen as a land where the repressive De la Garza family tradition will be unlikely to maintain its grip on the family.

5. Style

Magic Realism

It has been said that the role of magic realism eclipses any social realism the story might contain (*14*, p.102 and *19*, pp.189–190). Although Gabriel García Márquez's novel *Cien años de soledad* is most probably the one which sparked critics around the globe to comment on magic realism in the Latin American novel, it is certainly possible that it was the film of *Como agua* that exposed the greatest number to the theme. As mentioned previously, although *Como agua* was first conceived as a film script, then converted into a novel, only later to be translated to the screen; nonetheless, it is in the novel that the reader is able to find most examples of magic realism. In other words, magic realism is more authentically portrayed in the novel than in the film.

There are several ways in which a discussion of the use of magic realism comes into play. Franz Roh — the German art critic who coined the phrase — offers a discussion of how man's (and of course woman's) alienation and disorientation is important to magic realism. These are both themes that stand out in the narrative.

Though Franz Roh's actual influence on contemporary literary genre has been described as 'debatable',[12] several of his original ideas on what he calls 'this famous term' can be used to illuminate *Como agua*. In his initial writings, in which he wished to depart from

---

[12] Irene Guenther qualified Roh's current influence on literary genre as debatable due to the fact that his original pictorial formulations had become so transmuted by the time they were being used to refer to Latin American literary texts (*36*, p. 61). She speculates that this could possibly be due to problems linked to linguistic and cultural translations as well as 'the ambiguous meanings allocated to each of those two words [magic realism]' (*36*, p.62).

the idea of Post-Expressionism, Franz Roh wrote on magic realism as an idea which seems to oppose Surrealism. Roh explained that vitally important to the development of magic realism is the vision of 'man's alienation and disorientation' (*36*, p.38). Further commenting Roh by saying that much of magic realism has to do with the 'alienated individual placed in a modern world he can neither fathom nor control' (*36*, p.43). As we shall see, these themes are relevant to an analysis of *Como agua* and the theme of isolation will be discussed in greater depth later (see pp.83–87). More recently, magic realism has been defined as 'literature in which elements of the marvellous, mythical, or dreamlike are injected into an otherwise realistic story without breaking the narrative flow' (*43*, no pagination). This definition will help us as we look at magic realism's role in the story.

Part Two: The film

Alfonso Arau

Due to their divorce after the making of the film version of *Como agua*, considering the former couple together in any analysis has been unpopular. However the fact that this book studies both the film and the novel, makes it necessary to include them both. Alfonso Arau (b. 1932) has enjoyed a varied career as an actor, a director and a screenwriter. In the United States, he has appeared in films such as *The Three Amigos* (1986) and *Romancing the Stone* (1984), as well as in several episodes of Disney specials, and even in an episode of *Miami Vice*. In Mexico he has appeared in films such as *Camino largo a Tijuana* (1991) and *Calzonzín Inspector* (1974). Much like his acting, his work as a director has also taken place in the USA and Mexico, producing films such as *Zapata — El sueño del héroe* (2004) and *Tacos de oro* (1985) in his native Mexico (not to mention *Como agua* in 1992), and *A Walk in the Clouds* (1995) in the United States. On at least two of these projects he was also one of the writers: *Zapata — el sueño del héroe* and *Calzonzín Inspector* for example (*28*, no pagination). Such varied experience should make it no surprise that he was recently given the 'Luminaria Award', for the various achievements of his career, at the 2004 Santa Fe Film Festival. Nonetheless, one of his best-known films (and the one that has definitely received the most recognition) is the one considered here.

Here is a list of the film's cast and crew:

Cast

Main Cast

Tita – *Lumi Cavazos*

Pedro Muzquiz – *Rodolfo Arias*

John – *Mario Iván Martínez*

Doña Elena – *Regina Tome*

Rosaura – *Yareli Arizmendi*

Gertrudis – *Claudette Maillé*

Chencha – *Pilar Aranda*

Nacha – *Ada Carrasco*

Crew

Screenplay – *Laura Esquivel*

Producer – *Alfonso Arau*

Director – *Alfonso Arau*

Film Editing – *Carlos Bolando, Francisco Chiu*

Original Music – *Leo Brower*

Special Effects Supervisor – *Raul Falomir*

Costume and Wardrobe – *Victor Balderas, María Inés Gariby*

6. *Magic Realism on the Silver Screen*

As mentioned in the introduction, Laura Esquivel, a scriptwriter, first conceived the idea for this famous story as a film. After talking to various people about her idea, and the possibility of converting it into a feature film, she was discouraged from doing so and advised to write it as a novel. However, one might ask, why was this? Given the relatively smaller budgets (when compared to other film industries) which Mexican directors are given to work with, one might guess that the suggestion to turn the film into a novel was to do with the amount of magic realism Esquivel integrates into her storyline. Special effects can be costly in any film. When one watches the film, it is evident that one of the differences between the novel and the film is the way in which these are portrayed. It is impossible to know exactly why this is so, but it could be due to economic factors. In the cinematic version of Laura Esquivel's story it would be fair to say that the magical-realist events have been toned down and, in some cases, eliminated altogether. This next section will consider several magical-realist events and how they are portrayed in the film, as this is one of the significant ways in which the text varies from the film.

One of the ways in which Esquivel sets the tone for the film with regard to magic realism is its presence from the outset. The film opens with the birth of Tita. While her mother and Nacha are chopping onions in the kitchen, Tita is crying in her mother's womb (presumably from the eye-watering smell of the onions). Tita's copious tears literally push her from the womb into the world, as her mother gives birth, extremely quickly, on the kitchen table. The clearing of the kitchen table by Mamá Elena is very dramatic, as she flings several items onto the floor before lying down on it. The father runs in just as Tita emerges into the world and the camera captures her birth in a tilt shot from one of the lower corners of the room, taking maximum advantage of the huge amounts of water that pour off the table onto the floor and down the stairs. During this whole sequence violins are violently building tension in the soundtrack. The scene is very similar to the one in the novel (though one might have expected more water). However, the film appears to amplify the magical event by magnifying the amount of salt left over from the mixture of Tita's tears and the amniotic fluid drying in the sun. It suggests the amount is roughly four times greater than stated in the book. Stephen Hart has proposed that the suggestion that this salt was used for cooking is a part of the magic realism (5, p.174). It is magical yes, and possibly slightly stomach-churning as well.

The next significant magical-realist event in the film has to do with the baking and eating of the wedding cake by Tita and Nacha. While being forced to bake Rosaura's wedding cake, Tita — realising that she is finally alone with her true confidant, Nacha — cries over the batter. Tears spill into the mixture and she is then sent to bed by her mentor so as not to make the batter unusable: 'no chilles sobre la masa porque luego no va a servir'. These words prove to be a foreshadowing of future events. In her final shot as a living character we see Nacha taste the batter (as if to wonder what effect Tita's tears will have on the mixture) and then we do not know what becomes of her until after the wedding. As the relationship between Tita and salt has already been established, her salty tears in the batter could also be another symbolic motif, suggesting Tita herself entering the batter. The next scene, which includes the wedding feast the two cooks have prepared, takes place outside — Nacha has disappeared — when the dinner has ended and Chencha is serving the wedding cake. Nostalgic *norteña* music plays in the background as the guests chat amongst themselves, not expecting the events which are about to take place — though we are expecting something to happen, thanks to Nachas's warning about Tita's tears. Whilst Nacha's warning is useful, inasmuch as it puts us on guard about what might be going to happen with the batter, the tear effects are also useful in several ways. In creating this magical moment we can see how the director builds up the tension. As we watch a piece of the magical cake passed from guest to guest, served along the very long and narrow table (a good use of panning technique), we begin to

realise its importance. At about the same time, a strange wind begins
to blow. It is as if the magic blows in, and this is effective because
the wind is naturally linked to the supernatural. It is something that
can be heard, and its force can be seen and felt, but the wind is
invisible. The same can be said for the magic operating here. So, in
order to help us 'see', the narrator tells us what is happening (as in
the novel). She explains before leaving the scene (while we watch
Tita walking past the guests — as if to suggest that it is she who is
touching their lives at this moment — while robbing the moment
from the bride, her sister) that as the guests begin to eat the cake,
they begin to feel enormous nostalgia for the one they have loved.
Through the eating of the cake, Tita is forcing them to empathise
with her plight, though it is the narrator who explains the magical
effects. However, the scene ends with everyone vomiting into the
river, or wherever they can. The magic of the episode is only evident
thanks to a combination of two visual prompts — the wind, and
Tita's actions — but our viewing it as magic depends largely on the
narration of the events. It is of course after this event that we
discover that the one who tries the batter in its rawest form, Nacha,
has actually died from its effects. Whether this is due to her advanced
age, or to the potency of the batter in its uncooked form, one can only
guess. It is in this episode in the film too, that we can see Mamá
Elena pining over her secret mulatto lover for the first time (he will
not be introduced into the novel until some time later).

Perhaps the most famous and memorable of all the magical-
realist events is that of the quail in rose sauce. After receiving a
bouquet of roses from Pedro on her first anniversary as the De la
Garza ranch cook, Tita is ordered to throw them away because they
have upset her sister Rosaura (presumably because they were not
given to her). When she is about to fulfil her mother's order, Nacha's
voice tells her to use them to make the rose petal sauce which in the
book is supposedly an ancient Aztec recipe — although roses are
said to have been brought over by the Spanish. This is one of the
reasons why the miracle of Juan Diego having his *tilma* full of roses
is so significant. Perhaps this lack of agreement is the reason why it

does not appear in the film version.[13] She duly makes the rose petal sauce and serves it with quail. The book explains that one of the reasons for the magical effects of Tita's cooking is because she cooks with love. She uses food as her only way of showing Pedro that she loves him, and whilst we do see her cooking for Pedro, in the film it is difficult to see how she puts love into her dishes. It is clear that she is happy while making meals, but that is all, and the narrator does not give us more details. We are simply supposed to remember what she once tells Paquita: 'el secreto está en que cuando lo cocine, lo haga con mucho amor'. However, in the film, this idea of creating dishes with love does have effects which everyone can see.

As the family sits around the table and eats the meal, we begin to see its effects. As in the novel, several of them comment on the meal, and this helps us to perceive the magic. Rosaura declares that she feels bad, and Mamá Elena says it is too salty (though secretly she enjoys the meal — something omitted from the film — Mamá Elena is more interested in appearances than in the truth). Pedro is unable to contain himself and exclaims, in words from the novel, '¡Esto, es un placer de los dioses!' (p.50). This is the beginning of the magic, which is starting to work thanks to the special meal. Once again, the narrator is necessary for us to be sure of the workings of the dinner. She explains that the food has caused a unique form of communication between Pedro and Tita, in which Tita actually enters Pedro through the food. It is suggested that by eating the quail in rose sauce he experiences Tita carnally. The person who synthesizes all of this, explains the narrator, is Gertrudis, who also shows us that she is eroticized by the meal. The camera films her in close up as she rips open her dress to expose her ample cleavage, pushes her breasts up sensually and then makes her way down below, where the camera cannot see her hands, though it is suggested that she is touching herself erotically.

It is at this point that the camera focuses exclusively on Gertrudis. We see her run to take a shower because she has become

---

[13] The Juan Diego and the Virgin of Guadalupe miracle are succinctly narrated and explored in D. Brading's study of this virgin's image in *Mexican Phoenix* (*31*, pp.55–75).

extremely 'hot' — an easy connection with the Spanish idea of hot = sexually excited — and she wants to cool down. However, unlike in the novel, where Gertrudis is so hot that the water evaporates even before it touches her, the water does actually stream over her body, and soon the heat which is emanating from her causes the shower-house to burst into flames. At this point she runs from the ranch, to be swept away by the general who becomes her first love, and later her husband. Apart from telling us how Pedro and Tita's love is combined in Gertrudis, on this occasion the narrator leaves us to work out just how magical this event is. While such links are not hard to make, the event is not emphasized as much in the cinematic version as in the text.

While this magical-realist scene is not quite as prominent as in the novel, others are narrated in a way that is just as matter-of-fact. For example, when Rosaura is unable to produce milk for her first born son Roberto, she hands him over to Tita (much like Mamá Elena did with Tita when she was born). However, unlike Nacha, who gave Tita teas and *atoles*, Tita is 'magically' able to breastfeed the child even though her breast is 'virgin'. An episode which is reminiscent of Unamuno's *La tía Tula* (1921), in which an aunt (like Tita) also breastfeeds a child when she herself is still a virgin, is presented to us in Arau's film as simply another happening. The novel underlines the magic of it far more, and even describes her as 'Ceres — la diosa de la comida' (p.77). Perhaps this downplaying of Tita's breastfeeding of Roberto is because, scientifically speaking, it is not so magical after all.[14] Likewise however, the birth of Roberto, which is quite magical in the sense that Nacha talks Tita through it, is simply reduced to Tita's invoking Nacha by yelling her name, though she is then seen praying to the virgin Mary. We are unable to see the magical help she receives from beyond.

Another magical-realist episode, which is only hinted at in the film version of *Como agua*, is the final argument between Rosaura and Tita. In the book, we witness the fight between the two rivals

---

[14] Judith Lauwers and Anna Swisher's study *Counseling: The Nursing Mother* explains how adoptive and other non-birth mothers can breastfeed babies and young children (*42*, p.452).

(which is to be the final one both in the book and in the film, though in the book others are referred to). Possibly it is chosen because of its highly magical qualities, or possibly because it is after this fight that everything becomes clear — Pedro's and Tita's relationship is established and the secret love triangle is dissolved, though the three will continue to live together, on different terms, until Rosaura's death: Rosaura is the 'official wife', the 'official mother' and, the 'official teacher' of her daughter; but Tita is Pedro's lover and sentimental companion, the family cook and the unofficial teacher of Esperanza. This quarrel is important because, in a way, it is the quarrel which sets out the division of labour for the rest of their lives. It is also possible that this event in the novel is closely narrated because it is the most magical of all the confrontations. Several of these come into play in this episode. As the argument escalates between the two sisters, the baby Esperanza begins to cry more and more loudly, until her screaming reaches colossal proportions. The negative energy from the fight somehow transfers itself to a group of chickens which Tita is feeding (another relationship between food and magic). Perhaps the negative energy she feels is transferred into the *tortillas* she is ripping up (an aggressive action as well). The chickens begin to fight 'like fighting cocks' — an interesting comment, suggesting that the women are acting like men. The birds begin to chase one another so vigorously that they kick up a tornado, which carries away every thing in its path, including Esperanza's nappies, and threatens to take Tita as well. What is left are a few 'one-eyed hens'. Even the symbolism of the one-eyed hens is significant. They seem to symbolise how, after this argument in which both sisters come clean about their relationship with Pedro, they agree to turn a blind eye to what the other is doing as long as it is kept secret from others. This is a sad comment. Both, like the one-eyed hens who are left in the wake of the tornado and the chicken fight, are left on the ranch in the ruins of what remains after the quarrel, a grim image indeed. However, most of the magic realism and other symbolism is lost in the film's fight scene. We see the two women fighting near the chicken coop while Tita is preparing the

The sisters' final on-screen confrontation

tortillas for them. However, apart from having words with each other, airing their feelings, and agreeing on future relations at the De la Garza home, that is all that happens. Esperanza's crying appears to be the event that ends the argument, but she does not cry as extremely as in the written text either.

The only moment when magic is even hinted at occurs after Rosaura leaves the screen, and we see Tita, the barn where she was feeding the chickens, and the cloth nappies hanging out to dry. The camera takes a brief moment of reflection to film the scene of the fight, and the same magical wind appears to blow through the nappies, causing them to sway. We hear it blow just as in the episode when the magical cake is served and eaten at Rosaura's wedding. The scene seems to set itself up for a magical segment, but it does not fulfil its promise — or perhaps it is simply a reference to what happens in the book. It is somewhat unclear why this is not developed further but, given the prohibitive cost of special effects at the time the film was made, creating the novel's tornado would have been neither cheap nor easy.

In the film, Rosaura's death is also portrayed with a minimum of magic. Whereas in the book we read that her constant flatulence shakes the house, making the lights flicker, and even causing Pedro to wonder if the neighbours are having car trouble, we simply hear quite innocuous farting coming from Rosaura's room. It sounds so normal that it requires the narrator to tell us that it is Rosaura's excessive wind that causes her death. Likewise, the film does not allow us to see her burial — plagued by vultures following the awful stench. Perhaps such a comic magical-realist episode was thought to be too crude for film audiences, and therefore omitted.

As at the beginning of the film, the magical episode depicted at the end does not disappoint. After the wedding between Alex and Esperanza finishes, everyone leaves them alone — owing to the magical effects of the *chiles en nogada*. Finally Pedro and Rosaura are able to express their love with unbridled passion, which causes the ranch to go up in flames. There are a few scenes in the novel which do not take place in the film: while we do see Nacha lighting candles in the dark room (suggesting that their dark relationship can now be revealed to others by her shedding light on it) she does not disappear into the air as in the book. Likewise, while Tita does throw her huge knitted quilt around both her and Pedro, it does not cover the whole ranch as in the novel. — the idea that the quilt covers the whole ranch is significant, as it could be interpreted as the wick which helps the fire to destroy Tita's prison. The quilt itself could be interpreted as the material symbol of the lack of affection which Tita feels, the cold from which she suffers because of Pedro's absence from her life and the nervous energy she feels because of her lack of love. She wants something to keep her hands occupied at night, and as a substitute for sex she knits to keep herself busy. However, the starting of the fire, and the meeting of the two in the tunnel, is the same in the film as in the novel and its dramatic portrayal is effective. The fire begins in the room, spreads to the couple, and then extends to the whole ranch as we witness its dramatic destruction. The visual effects are effective and, as already discussed, their symbolism is important. The only significant events omitted are the ranch turning into a volcano (a symbol of voluptuous femininity) and the amount of ash left after the fire turning it into an Eden-like place. These are the final effects of the couple leaving their family home.

The final destruction of the De la Garza ranch

When considering why certain magical-realist scenes are shortened or eliminated in the film, it is difficult to reach a conclusion. While comparing the two versions helps to see material that has been lost or eliminated (such as symbolism, subtexts, different aspects of relationships and messages implicit in the written text); it does not offer any clear solutions as to why parts have been cut or otherwise modified. Nor does the technical difficulty of a magical-realist scene appear always to influence why certain things are not portrayed. For example, the magical elements of Rosaura's death are quite simple, but are downplayed in the cinematic version. What is true is that in taking a novel and turning it into a film, elements are often lost — though this one does lose less than others. That said, a comparative analysis shows us that, above all, this is a film about love, about the relationship between Pedro and Tita, and about the ranch and the food served there. When it came to removing certain elements of the novel, these were seen to be the film's defining themes. Indeed, it is the narrative, and not the magic, which is used to frame the film.

7. Isolation

As mentioned in part one in relation to magic realism, on at least four different occasions the camera pans back and one is able to contemplate the ranch in a way which does not occur in the book. What we see is a striking view of the De la Garza ranch in what appears to be complete isolation. This depiction of the ranch is impressive, and suggests many different reasons as to why it was filmed in this way.

Firstly one can see the De la Garza ranch as a microcosm of Mexico (many elements of society pass though its doors). However, given the unusual events on the ranch, it is even more likely that this isolation is being used to underline the differences that exist between Mamá Elena's home and wider Mexican society. It is ruled by women (at a time when Mexico is dominated by men). It holds a strange tradition, by which the youngest daughter is bound to take care of the mother until death (a tradition not normally found in Mexican society at that time, or at any other time). Magical events related to food take place there. This depiction of the family home seems to suggest that it is a law unto itself, slightly separated from society. However, this is not the only way of interpreting the ranch and its place in the film and novel.

The ranch can be seen in two ways: either as a kind of flawed *locus amoenus*[15] or as a prison. The ranch is a *locus amoenus* in as much as it is the meeting place of the two main lovers, Tita and Pedro. It is here that they meet, where their first declaration of love occurs, and where they finally consummate their love. It is the place of encounter of Tita's sisters as well. Both Gertrudis and Rosaura meet their partners at the ranch and both have their first sexual

---

[15] From Greek and Latin literature, an idyllic place where lovers meet (*33*, p.619).

encounters there — though for Rosaura it is more the fulfilling of
marital duty to Pedro. Gertrudis is literally picked up from the ranch
and carried from it during her first encounter. However, the family
home is far from the ideal one would expect with of a *locus amoenus*.
It does have a river which flows by it (though its only use in the film
is for the guests to vomit into after eating Rosaura's wedding cake,
and for the bandits who rape Chencha and disable Mamá Elena to use
as a point of arrival). Far from being full of leafy trees, there are
hardly any trees at all, and those that are there are thin and
uninteresting. There is vegetation, but it is mostly desert scrub:
cactus and suchlike. While there is something picturesque about the
site, it is not Eden-like in its appearance.

        The other aspect of the location is that, for both Tita and
Rosaura, the ranch seems to suggest that it is the place where lovers
meet but are not fulfilled. Whilst Gertrudis leaves the ranch, and her
belonging to it is denied by her mother, Rosaura and Tita live out
most, if not all, of their relationship with Pedro there. However,
neither of them is satisfied with the relationship. Rosaura is unhappy
because she realises that her husband is not in love with her, and has
only chosen her in order to be close to Tita. Tita, on the other hand,
is dissatisfied with the relationship because she is unable to live her
love with Pedro to the fullest. Unable to show her love in public, she
is only able to demonstrate it to Pedro through food, and much later
through secret meetings in 'the dark room', where they fear being
overheard.

        As mentioned above, another way of interpreting the ranch,
helped by its isolation in the film, is to see it as a prison. Separated
from the rest of the world, and built close to the edge of a cliff, the
De la Garza ranch makes one think of a citadel, or a fortress on a
cliff; it is like a castle or a tower which is erected either for
protecting one from, or for preventing one from accessing, the
outside world. There are those who come and go, such as the priest
or the local busybody, Paquita Lobo, but for those who either work
for the De la Garza family or who are born into it, leaving the ranch
permanently does not appear to be an option. The only viable way
out appears to be death or exile — either temporary or permanent. Of

the three sisters, only Gertrudis leaves the ranch for good. She is allowed to escape when she is carried off by the revolutionary soldier; however it could be argued that her exit from the ranch is possible because she was never officially part of the family — as she is illegitimate. Both Rosaura and Tita, true De la Garza daughters, remain tied to the ranch. Rosaura spends some time far from the ranch in San Antonio, Texas (where her son dies). However, when her mother dies, Rosaura immediately returns, the trauma of the occasion inducing premature labour and the birth of the next generation (Esperanza) on the ranch. Pedro, Rosaura's husband, is likewise bound to the ranch, as it is his only way of being close to Tita.

Whatever one's interpretation of the ranch, Tita is the character who is most enslaved. From almost the first time that we see her (with Nacha, while the maid is cooking in the kitchen) it becomes apparent that she is trapped in Mamá Elena's home. Nacha is cooing to Tita as a baby, telling her how beautiful she is, and how she will easily be married when she grows older. Mamá Elena stops her immediately, and prohibits her from giving Tita the idea that she will ever leave the ranch, because of the family tradition. For others, it appears, the possibility of leaving might exist, but Tita will be tied to the ranch until the day of her mother's death. What is interesting is that, even after her mother dies, Tita remains at the De la Garza home. It is true that she is free to leave the ranch, but she does not go. Thus Mamá Elena's power over the family is enough to keep it imprisoned even after her death.

There is a time though, when Tita is able to escape Mamá Elena's grasp. After losing her mind when her young nephew dies, Tita is sent out of Mexico to a mental asylum (though, as mentioned above, Dr Brown does not send her there). It is important to underline that it is Mamá Elena's decision to remove Tita from the ranch, in the same way as it is her decision to send Rosaura and Pedro to San Antonio. Like a jailer, she is the one who decides who will leave and when. What is significant is that they all return to their home/prison when their jailer is attacked by bandits. Later, it appears to be the love triangle, Tita-Pedro-Rosaura, a sense of family responsibility, and the idea of 'keeping up appearances' that keeps them on the ranch.

Within the ranch there are many prisons as well. These are prisons in the sense that the characters find spaces to lock themselves away from, or to hide from, others who might be controlling them. However, these are spaces that the characters enter voluntarily. For example, the dark room, the 'cuarto oscuro', is first used by Mamá Elena and Tita for bathing Mamá Elena. Later, however, it becomes the secret location used by Pedro and Tita to enjoy sexual relations. Similarly, the pigeon loft is used by Tita when she wishes to lock herself away from Mamá Elena after the death of Rosaura's son. This too could be viewed as a type of prison.

There are a few moments when escape from their home/prison is suggested. When discovering that Tita may be pregnant, Pedro suggests that the couple run away from the ranch and find somewhere else to live. However, it is Tita who convinces Pedro that they must stay within the confines of the ranch, so that he may fulfil his responsibilities to his daughter and his wife.

The idea of the De la Garza ranch as a prison is also reinforced by the end of *Como agua*. In the last love scene between Tita and Pedro, we see the couple finally able to express their love without the worry that anyone will discover their secret. This is not because they reveal their relationship to the world — though it is suggested that they will do so as Pedro has asked Tita to marry him — but rather because 'no one can hear them' (reinforcing the Christian notion that this type of relationship is sinful, and that they should feel shame for what they are doing). In this final encounter, Pedro and Tita, after experiencing so many years of frustration, climax so intensely that the tunnel Dr Brown has warned them about (when explaining about the book of matches everyone has inside them) appears, and Pedro enters it. Tita, upon learning that Pedro has gone through the tunnel, decides to go through it too. It is at this moment that the lovers are finally free from the ranch, and it is at this moment also that the novel describes them as having gone to their real *locus amoenus*, 'el edén perdido' (p.246). At the same time, the ranch goes up in flames — a celebration of their love, but also the destruction of the ranch. The burning of the family home symbolises the end of Mamá Elena's power over the couple, as well as the end of the family tradition and the freedom of Tita and Pedro. Its destruction allows the reader to see that Tita's promise that the family tradition will end with her, is fulfilled. Not only does Tita not have children, thus eliminating the possibility of having a youngest daughter, but the niece she helped to raise is now married, and the ranch, where this strange family tradition held sway, has been destroyed.

8. The Ranch

When considering the use of the house, and how it is portrayed in *Como agua*, it is relevant to comment on the different periods in which the camera focuses on it. This will help us to understand how these scenes reinforce some of the ideas we have been discussing.

(2:02) Just after the opening scene, in which Tita is born amidst her floods of tears, we see that the house is set in the past (a title tells us it is 1910). We can also see that it is separate from the town and has no close neighbours. However, about three and a half minutes later we have the first example of what might be called the 'isolation shot': a view of the ranch perched on a cliff and protected on one side by a river. It reinforces the impression of a fortress or prison as discussed above. Perhaps it is implying that Mamá Elena's territory is effectively separated from the world. In the shot, apart from vegetation, there is no visible life to be seen around the ranch. There are no birds in the air, no animals can be seen and there are no people in sight. It is during this first full view of the De la Garza ranch that the narrator (Tita's grand-niece) tells us of Tita's childhood, and what it was that she did while she was growing up — mostly she speaks of food and cookery. Talking of Tita's childhood while we see the ranch in the midst of its isolation suggests that the narrator wants to underline the fact that Tita is trapped there, and bound to its kitchen.

The next view we have of the house (13:31) is when Tita learns that her boyfriend is to marry her sister and not herself. Surrounded by darkness, and lit only by a full moon, the house is dark, except for a small light in Tita's room. It is against this background that the narrator begins to describe the void which Tita feels inside, and how this emptiness may be compared to a 'black-hole', engulfing all emotion. The darkness surrounding this lonely home in the country

A view of the secluded ranch

complements the mood of the protagonist, reinforcing the tragedy of the situation. She appears trapped in her mother's home.

One interesting shot of the ranch shows Gertrudis' escape. Whilst Gertrudis escapes the ranch fairly early on, and it has been argued that this is possible partly because she is not of the De la Garza line, but rather the daughter of Mamá Elena's mulatto lover, her escape from the ranch in the film is worthy of comment. When Gertrudis attempts to take a shower after eating the quail in rose sauce, we see her run out of the burning shower-house and up towards and past a barn, which appears to mark the outer limit of the ranch. In order to reach the barn she has to run up the small hill upon which it is located. While she runs, slightly tense music is played, as if to show the triumph of one of the sister's attempts to gain her freedom. As she passes the outer limits of the ranch she is met by a general in the revolutionary army, who picks her up and carries her away. She only returns after the death of the mother, and then only for short visits, as when she is drawn there to eat her favourite foods, to give Tita advice while recovering her childhood, and to attend her niece's wedding.

At the same time as Gertrudis' escape is taking place (30:36) (the novel states that Tita's and Pedro's love is synthesized in and through Gertrudis), and unbeknown to her, Tita and Pedro are looking on and they re-enact the scene they have just witnessed.

Pedro, like the general, also has a vehicle in the scene; it is a bicycle and, like the general, he appears to want to put Tita on it and ride away with her to some untold destination. However Pedro is the general's foil. While the general is strong, tall and has a big moustache, Pedro is small, bourgeois, and clean-shaven. The general has a large horse and rides it well, while Pedro wobbles around on his flimsy bicycle. While Pedro appears to represent modernity — he has all the latest technology and is polished in his appearance — it is the rustic general that the women need in order to escape from the ranch. What Pedro's foil does have is good timing. The general arrives just in time to sweep Gertrudis off her feet and to carry her away in fairytale fashion. Pedro appears still to be wavering, waiting for Tita's final approval, when suddenly Mamá Elena appears and, again imposing her will, demands an explanation, thus frustrating Pedro's plans. The jailer has once more kept the couple within the limits of her metaphorical prison.

Another view of the ranch, which becomes significant, is the shot of the 'cuarto oscuro', previously used for Mamá Elena's bathing ritual. When, for reasons unknown to us, Tita enters this space, she is trapped by Pedro and he obliges her to have sex with him. The scene is significant because it appears to foretell the destruction of the ranch. As the two make love for the first time we, together with Rosaura and Chencha, see thunder and lightning threatening the ranch, and watch sparks fly from the dark room where the two lovers are carnally united. It is in this scene that the destruction of the ranch, through the union of Tita and Pedro, is foreshadowed. Immediately following the episode, there is another full view of the ranch (1:05:15). Once again the director shows it in a long shot from a distance. This impressive scene, underlining the isolation of the De la Garza home, is perfectly timed. Whereas Tita is due to leave the ranch forever, owing to her forthcoming marriage to Doctor Brown, the fact that she has lost her virginity to Pedro — and, worse still, that she believes she is expecting his baby — seems once more to have condemned her to stay. Since Tita does not want to run away with Pedro, she is left in a submissive position, locked into the love triangle between herself, Pedro and Rosaura. This compositional shot of the lonely ranch from afar seems to assure us that Tita's place on the ranch has been secured.

This idea of the sisters being locked in a love triangle because they are bound by society and their family home to keep up appearances becomes evident in a quarrel they have on the patio. Not unlike two prisoners who pick a fight in the prison courtyard, once Rosaura becomes aware that Pedro and Tita are having an affair she confronts Tita in the yard. There they argue about several things, and finally agree that Tita can do what she likes with Pedro as long as it remains secret. Again, appearances are the only things that seem to matter to Rosaura. Tita appears to accept the terms, but what is significant in this sequence is that, for almost the whole time they are arguing, the De la Garza home is fully centred in the background. It is as if we are watching the two sisters argue about their location. It also seems to suggest that the ranch is what has brought the two women together and, in the same way, it is the only thing that is keeping them together. Even though Mamá Elena is dead, her home appears to be keeping a watchful eye on the women, ensuring that they are unable to leave its confines.

In the final minutes of the film we see the ranch for the last time. In darkness, after Esperanza's wedding has taken place, we watch Tita and Pedro walk through the ranch, not realising that it will be for the last time. It is night and they are alone, and as they enter the dark room to make love (one has to ask why they do not make love in the house if it is finally theirs) they realise that the room has been prepared by Nacha's ghost, which discreetly fades away as they enter. The dark room has been lit by hundreds, if not thousands, of candles. The couple's *cuarto de pecado* has become a romantic trysting place, ablaze with light from this multitude of small flames. While they undress and prepare to give themselves to each other, the camera cross-cuts between the couple and the ranch outside. Though they are unaware of it, as they prepare to make love thunder and lightning dance around the ranch, threatening to destroy it. Finally, having made love freely for the first time, both are able to see the magical tunnel which appeared when Tita stayed with Dr Brown. Once they are finally reunited in it (Tita having struggled to get back to it, after having turned away), the ranch bursts into flame and burns until nothing remains except Tita's cookery book. The couple have escaped the prison/ranch and enjoy their love in another extremely mundane place. The destruction of the ranch through Tita and Pedro's love is significant. One cannot help but compare the biblical destruction of cities with the dramatic end of the De la Garza ranch. Like a strange retelling of the destruction of Sodom and Gomorrah (Gen. 19), the De la Garza ranch is destroyed as a result of the sensuality and fornication of Tita and Pedro. However, unlike the biblical account, in this reworking of the story their destruction is welcomed and, to an extent, even desired because it coincides with their escape. It is as if once the two last inhabitants have left, fire and brimstone rain down until nothing remains, thus ensuring that the curse (of the youngest daughter who is denied love) will be broken forever. A more romantic reading of the ending would suggest that the couple's intense passion creates so much heat that it causes the ranch to be consumed, and to go up in smoke, just as they are so consumed by their own love and pleasure that they too are transported to a different plane. Whichever interpretation of the conclusion is more appropriate, it is clear that our last view of the ranch is of destruction and desolation. The prison walls are broken and the lovers are freed. The book then suggests a redemptive theme — once the ashes from the destruction of the ranch have settled then 'bajo las cenizas floreció todo tipo de vida, convirtiendo ese terreno en el más fértil de la región' (p.247). This reaction, too, is a retelling of the Sodom and Gomorrah story; however, instead of nothing growing after its destruction, the ranch becomes full of life. So from the destruction of their home, what was a prison for the De la Garza family (or, at best, a failed garden of Eden) becomes a fruitful garden, perhaps even a garden of Eden on the border of northern Mexico.

9. Genre-Specific Elements

The clothing the different characters wear plays a specific role in the film. As it is set around the turn of the century, initially in the 1910s and later in the 1930s, the clothing has been selected to suit Mexicans of that era. In addition, as different classes are represented, so is their clothing distinct. As most people in the film are from the up-and-coming, if not wealthy, classes, they appear in the typical attire of the day. The servants wears appropriate clothing, as do the revolutionaries; even the bandits' clothing has been carefully selected to fit their role. However, although all are dressed as we would expect, there are important distinctions which can be demonstrated, and which help us better to understand the film and the messages it wishes to convey. The distinctions of clothing also make statements about the characters, their place in the story and their relationship to each other.

The servants, Nacha and Chencha, who are vital to the story line, are dressed in unflattering, nondescript dark-coloured and worn clothes, which are almost always covered by a plain white apron (though with a few exceptions, such as when Chencha wears a nice, though dark and unflattering, traditional servant's dress while serving at Rosaura's wedding). Their clothes are not only a visual reminder of their class — they are poor servants of humble origins — it also distances them from the family in such a way as to tell them, and us that, while they are part of the household, they do not belong to it. However, notwithstanding these women's place within the home as a social structure, there are ways in which the non-belonging or non-importance is challenged, and there are a few instances when clothing is a visual clue to this. Because Nacha nursed Tita, this allows her to become a kind of surrogate mother to her. Likewise, the

time spent in the kitchen in her youth allows Tita to create a bond
with Nacha that is stronger than the one with her own mother. An
example of this bond can be found in a scene where we see Tita as a
child. Here we see both Nacha and Tita working together in the
kitchen. The music and the joy in the actresses' faces, as if they are
mother and daughter, is reinforced by the fact that they are both
wearing very similar clothing. This mirroring of each other by
dressing in the same way, helps to underline the strong bond that has
grown between them.

On the other hand, when it comes to the way in which Mamá
Elena and Tita are portrayed, the opposite effect is achieved. Apart
from the fact that they rarely work together, unless Mamá Elena is
helping with some aspect of the cooking, both Tita and Mamá Elena
dress quite differently. All of the women wear dresses throughout the
film, the De la Garza family and Paquita Lobos wear especially nice
ones — helping to denote their upper class status. This reflects the
styles which were common at the time. In the film however, Tita
dresses in clothing which almost always tends to be light in colour,
lacy and feminine. Her clothing is not overtly sexual by twentieth-
century standards, but it is visually attractive. The only exception to
Tita's light coloured wardrobe is what she wears when she is in
mourning, for example after the deaths of Nacha and Mamá Elena.
The only other time we see her wearing dark clothing is on the day
that her mother is attacked by bandits and perhaps this can be seen as
a foreshadowing of Mamá Elena's death. Mamá Elena, like Lorca's
Bernarda Alba on whom she is based is, by contrast, almost
exclusively portrayed in dark clothing. Whereas Tita is seen as
having a light-hearted personality, made to love, mother, cook, and
nurture, Mamá Elena is dark, unloving, cruel, vindictive and not at
all motherly. Throughout the film we see Mamá Elena in many
circumstances, and the only one where she is wearing noticeably
light-coloured, and somewhat feminine, clothing is in the opening
scene, when she is about to give birth to Tita. At this point, her
husband is still alive and it is possible that she dresses in this way
because her situation is different. However, the next time we see her,
Mamá Elena is wearing dark clothes, which is normal for people in

mourning, but which becomes her standard dress. Though almost always dark, it is not always black and she does wear outfits such as a black skirt with a black trimmed white shirt, or clothing which is grey or dark blue. There are a few exceptions, for example when the bandits chase her she is not wearing dark clothing, but she does cover herself with a dark shawl which emphasises her dark personality. It is interesting to note that on the occasion when we see Mamá Elena naked, while she is being bathed by Tita, it is in the supposition that she is in the *el cuarto oscuro*/the dark room. Watching the scene, we are silent intruders on a special, private ritual — her bathing by her servant daughter Tita. So again, it is under the cover of supposed darkness that she shields herself from the gaze of the world.

If Tita is depicted as being Nacha's adopted daughter, by dressing like her in a scene from her childhood, Rosaura too is portrayed in the film as Mamá Elena's daughter by the way in which she dresses. The truth is that both the film and the book tell us very little about the relationship between the two. We do know; however, that she is the only true De la Garza girl to be free, and that she inherits the family ranch (as well as the ability to continue its traditions). In many ways her mother sets her up to live a life which mirrors her own. She is made to marry a man of her parent's choosing, lives on the ranch and learns to accept what she does not like in the name of appearing decent in the eyes of society. This is reflected in the clothing Rosaura wears. As if to say that she is the continuation of Mamá Elena, she too wears dark clothing almost exclusively. There are a few exceptions to this, mainly when she is married and complying with society's expectations — not to do so might lend itself to gossip. Also, when we see Rosaura in her night clothes, they are white in accordance with convention.

Perhaps both Mamá Elena and Rosaura wear dark clothes in order to show us that they are bad while Tita is good. It is a simple way of separating the two rival groups and allowing the audience to take sides.

Gertrudis' clothing is also quite significant in the film. In the first half we see her in what could be considered normal feminine clothing, wearing pastel coloured dresses which are quite flattering.

However, after she runs off with the *Villista* (which she does naked — perhaps symbolizing the shedding of her mother's, and society's, conventions) she does not come back for a long time. During this period, wondering if she is still going naked, Tita even sends her clothes. Nonetheless, when we see Gertrudis again she is wearing clothing very different from that of the other women. Although she still wears a skirt, she is also wearing more masculine items. She wears hats, waistcoats, jackets and a bandana in a way which flatters her, but does have a certain manliness (or at least a non-feminine look) about it. This way of dressing helpfully signals to us that Gertrudis is now a very non-traditional female for the time. As a *generala* in the *Villista* army she does not fit the usual stereotypes, nor does her dress allow her to look like a woman of the period. Just as the revolution changes, so does Gertrudis' clothing, but then again so does her husband's. In the final scene, in which we see Juan Alejandrez and Gertrudis, they appear to be quite settled, and even stylish and bourgeois in their clothing, and in the expensive motor car they are driving. The middle sister is once again wearing very feminine clothing — perhaps suggesting that the other modes she adopted were just temporary adaptations required by the Revolution.

The clothing that the men in *Como agua* wear is also worthy of comment. As this is a story about women, there are actually few male characters upon which to comment and, interestingly enough, those that are portrayed, appear to be from same mould. They all wear suits, and often top hats or bowlers for more formal occasions. Their stylish suits not only denote their status in society — they are upper class; not only can they afford the suits, because they are not required to do physical labour they can wear them as everyday clothing. This uniform-like attire also has the effect of making them blend into the background, not drawing undue attention to themselves. Even the priest is wearing standard attire for priests in Mexico at the time. Nothing appears to indicate that he is special in his status or order. He is just an ordinary priest (with a few hidden extra-curricular activities as discussed on pp.110–11). This is underlined by the number of times Pedro, who needs to stand out from the others, is dressed in a much lighter-coloured suit than other men in the film.

The uniform-like blandness of the latter's clothing (as well as their lack of dialogue in the film) indicates that the director ranks acting and script higher than costume.

There are two men who do have significant dialogue, and whose physical presence does need to be underlined in the film — Dr Brown and Pedro. Whilst both wear the standard suit for most of the film, there are a few ways in which they stand out. We have already mentioned that Pedro often wears a light-coloured suit — which helps to make him look polished and youthful — perhaps as the trophy husband whom Mamá Elena has obtained for her daughter Rosaura. The light-coloured suit also further emphasises the fact that, as a kind of kept man, he does not have to work and can wear such clothing because he is unlikely to dirty it. Dr Brown is often noticeable precisely because he does work (as a matter of fact he is the only man — apart from the hired hands and the priest — who is seen to work for a living. As a result, we often see Dr Brown without his coat and tie, and with the sleeves of his white shirt rolled up as he attends to a patient in the De la Garza home, or in his own home. This different attire focuses attention on him rather than other men in the film.

Similarly, when comparing Pedro and Dr Brown, we see other important differences and similarities between the two. For example, they are the only clean-shaven male actors. It is difficult to know exactly what this is supposed to mean, though we can make some educated guesses. It could be to appeal to European tastes and styles, and to make the leading men more attractive to a female audience, or possibly to help link the two by their physical similarities. It could also be to make them seem different, and to stand out from the others. Or it could be something much simpler, perhaps trying to underline the fact that they are young, since both are portrayed with moustaches in the final scenes, when they are much older. Considering their hairstyles, there is an important difference between them. Pedro, even from a young age, is always seen with longish hair — dark, thick and somewhat unruly, though not messy and in fact rather stylish. His is more the classic *galán* look, and his unruly hair seems to suggest that his life also has unruly aspects to it — such as

his intentions with regard to Tita when marrying Rosaura, and his
love affair with Tita while living at the De la Garza ranch. On the
other hand, Dr Brown's blond hair is always kept well under control,
slicked down with what appears to be a generous portion of hair gel.
Not unlike Mexico's famous president, Benito Juárez, he parts his
hair from one side in a look which suggests seriousness, if not
nerdiness. Indeed, his hairstyle reflects the control he demonstrates
over his emotions and in his discipline as a doctor and scientist. The
neatness of his hair seems to reflect his own imperturbable
demeanour. A similar comment could be made about Mamá Elena
and Rosaura (who are often depicted with their hair tightly tied up,
symbolising their need to exert control) and Tita (whose loosely-kept
hair seems to hint at her desire for sexual liberation).

The other men in the film, where they are not of the same
social status as the protagonists, are dressed in a way which fits their
job description. The handymen wear grubby, nondescript clothing
and the revolutionaries wear standard federal army uniforms (the
Villistas wore Mexican *vaquero*-like clothing — which would have
been historically accurate [*39*, pp.486–487]). The two *Villistas* who
are highly significant to the story are Sergeant Treviño and Juan
Alejandrez. Both are initially depicted as revolutionary soldiers, but
by the end of the film they have changed. They too have adopted the
style of the upper and upper-middle classes in Mexico. We see them
both (even Sergeant Treviño, who can hardly read) more or less
integrated into Mexico's upper classes, something denoted by their
clothing and by their clearly invited presence at Esperanza's
wedding. Perhaps this change — as they are the only ones who
change significantly — is meant to suggest that the revolution does
change the lives of these two fortunate men for the better.

Chiaroscuro

Chiaroscuro, a technical term in Italian for the use of the contrast
between light and dark, is important to the film version of *Como
agua*. It can be seen in the contrasts of clothing and in the use of light
and darkness. A close examination of the film — especially in an
older VHS version — will reveal a striking use of light and darkness

to underline situations, and especially people. This is particularly true of Tita, who receives the lion's share of illumination.

One could argue that so many contrasts between black and white, light and darkness, are simply a by-product of making a film set in an era before electric light. The use of candles, and the fact that many scenes take place indoors (where natural light, or candle and/or lantern light are used) make it inevitable that shadows will abound, and that there will be a chiaroscuro effect. It is the presence of chiaroscuro which helps to lend an air of authenticity to the scenes. One would expect homes to be poorly lit at this time and for a number of smaller light sources to be the norm. Nonetheless, there are certain occasions when light is specifically thrown onto certain people to stress their importance to a scene. In the majority of cases these have to do with Tita and we will consider a few examples.

Contrasts of light and darkness during Rosaura's meal

When it comes to lighting, Tita is without a doubt the one who receives the most attention, and rightly so as she is the main character in the story. Her entrance into, and exit from, the ranch coincides with chiaroscuro moments. At the moment she is born, light pours in through a window into an otherwise darkened room, illuminating the lower half of Mamá Elena's body and the figure of Nacha, the

woman who will be Tita's practical and spiritual mother (2:49). This
particular scene, with the light focussing on her, points to her
importance to the narrative. (The magical salt residue, left after
Tita's birth, is also emphasised by the same technique 3:01).
Similarly, as the film is about to draw to a close, Tita and Pedro
leave the De la Garza ranch forever when they meet at the entrance
of their tunnel. This scene offers a beautiful play on light and
darkness, as we see the lovers silhouetted against the bright light
shining from the tunnel (1:41:38). It emphasises not only the final
union of the two soulmates, in what looks to be an eternal embrace,
but also the fact that they have finally escaped from the place which
appeared determined to keep them apart.

      There are several other instances when Tita is the object of
specific lighting against a dark background and we will look at a few
of them. (7:30) She is silhouetted against the background during the
scene where Pedro declares his eternal love for her — and he is
similarly brilliantly lit. (11:24) This shows a family portrait in which
all of the sisters, and Nacha and Chencha — who are arguably Tita's
adoptive mother and sister — are together. They are all lost in lesser
illumination — especially Rosaura who almost disappears into a dark
corner — except for Tita, who is bathed in light as she stands
elegantly, expecting to receive her mother's permission to marry
Pedro. (13:41) The lamplight plays on Tita in her dark room, while it
also underlines her sadness and dejection when she considers that her
sister is to marry the love of her life. (17:40) During the wedding
scene in the church, it is Tita's bench which is brightest in the poorly-
lit wedding chapel. (21:53) This frame contains a beautiful landscape
scene incorporating chiaroscuro. During the burial of Nacha, the
camera captures a stunning sunset, which contrasts with the dark
heavens and the dark earth, and a striking triangle of light appears to
break into the clouds. The base of the triangle illuminates the two
gravediggers and the sole mourner, Tita, as well as the sad yet
impressive tombstones standing out against the horizon. It gives the
impression that Nacha is ascending to a higher glory, whilst also
underlining the sadness of the moment. (24:55) This moment finds
the table at which Rosaura's first dinner is being served. Each

individual is illuminated in turn when they, somewhat unwillingly, take their first bite of the horribly cooked meal. (24:58–25:15) Interestingly, this is one of the few occasions where light and dark contrasts are used while eating, and they are employed while the family is eating Rosaura's meal rather than Tita's. (35:29) Finds Dr Brown and Tita illuminated while gazing at one another. Dr Brown is openly admiring her. (36:37) This is a classical scene, in which light is used to suggest that, while breastfeeding Roberto, Tita is a kind of Ceres — the goddess of food. (41:33) Tita and Pedro's first romantic encounter is also a scene that employs chiaroscuro, not only in the moonlight which shines on them from the left, but also in the contrast of their white clothing (a subtle reference to their innocence) against the dark wall of the house. (46:13) Sees Tita taking refuge in the pigeon loft on top of the ranch. A bright light from the door shines onto someone who has lost her wits. (1:02:41) The light shines once again on Tita and Dr Brown during the ceremony in which he asks officially for her hand in marriage, while Pedro disappears into the dark background. (1:03:53) A similar light illuminates Tita's face while she and Chencha are washing dishes outside. The candlelight emphasises her beauty and innocence, before being blown out by Pedro as they first make love in total darkness. (1:16:55) Here, while Juan accompanies Pedro in a serenade to Tita, they are silhouetted against the background by the light from the campfire. (1:29:50) John and Tita's faces are lit by a brilliant Mexican sunset, while John reaffirms his love for Tita and renews his offer to marry her. (1:40:24) Finally, in the moments before Tita and Pedro's final encounter in the tunnel of light, as she suddenly realises that she can meet Pedro in the tunnel, we see Tita illuminated by light which suddenly streams in through the window (rather unusually for a night scene).

While there are many other episodes in which chiaroscuro plays an important role, most of them tend to have the same purpose as the ones just considered. We have mentioned a few, such as when Pedro and Juan Alejandrez serenade Tita, and when John is talking to Tita and other members of the family at the De la Garza home. However, as suggested above, Tita is the one who is most affected by this play on light and darkness, and it serves several purposes. It underlines moments of sadness and of joy, such as when she learns that Pedro will marry Rosaura, and when Dr Brown asks for her hand in marriage. It is used to make her stand out from the other characters, as in scenes where she is in the kitchen with others, or at a gathering in her home. Chiaroscuro also has a romantic effect, highlighting Tita at important moments and enhancing her beauty, as when she is breastfeeding Roberto or cooking special dishes. It focusses our attention on important incidents, such as when Pedro and Rosaura share a brief but passionate kiss and embrace for the first time. Chiaroscuro also offers a touch of realism, given that *Como agua* is set during a period when candles, rather than electric lamps, were the only available domestic source of light.

Subtle Symbolism

Como agua uses subtle symbolism in a number of ways. Some of them are simple, such as the occasional glimpses of the barren landscapes, mirroring the harsh family conditions in which Tita is obliged to live, and emphasising that she too is barren — whether wilfully or symbolically — and will not have a child of her own blood. Others, mentioned previously (see pp. 62–64), are more complex, such as the presence of Freemasonry in the film. Most, if not all, of these visual aids are not present in the novel and require careful viewing to unravel their symbolic importance. The next section will examine a few examples of the subtle symbolism to be found in the film.

Food is portrayed symbolically. For example, in the final dish to be eaten, *chiles en nogada*, the male sexual organ is symbolised. The fact that these chiles are eagerly stuffed into the mouths of those at the wedding party, just before they become very sexually aroused, is an allusion which is unlikely to go unnoticed by the audience.

One of the most poignant scenes occurs when Mamá Elena and Tita are stuffing sausages (*chorizo*), and Chencha comes into the kitchen to announce the terrible news that Rosaura's son has died. We see Tita in the far corner at the left and Chencha towards the right hand corner. In the centre is Mamá Elena, who receives the bad

*Mamá Elena strategically placed between the severed pig's head
and the meat hook when learning of Roberto's death*

news with a look of indifference. However, the ugliness of the scene
is emphasised by the articles which frame Mamá Elena. To Mamá
Elena's left we see a severed pig's head on a hook, and to the right
we have meat hooks and sausages. Mamá Elena's hands are bloodied
with the sausage mixture. If we consider that Tita then accuses Mamá
Elena of having killed her grandson, by sending them to the USA, the
framing of Mamá Elena effectively underlines her identity as the
murderer. Surrounded by butcher's implements, the mother has
clearly sent her grandson to the slaughter.

Immediately after this scene, we see Tita run up to the pigeon
loft, where she locks herself away from her mother. We see her run
up the stairs holding a pail and, according to the book, in the bucket
is a baby pigeon that Tita has been mothering since the revolutionary
soldiers took all the other birds away (p.93). Tita feeds the bird until
it dies — perhaps over-compensating for her desire to mother and
feed the nephew she had previously been caring for. However, with
the death of both the pigeon and her nephew, Tita begins a process of
rebirth. After taking refuge in the one place her mother will not
follow her (because of her fear of heights), Tita flees to the other side

of the border with Dr Brown. There she is reborn as someone able to stand up to her mother, and to others, to a far greater degree than before. There is thus a phoenix motif evident in this part of the narrative. The death of the bird, and of Tita's nephew, leads to her rebirth as a new and independent person.

Music

One of the obvious ways in which the film differs from the book is in its incorporation of a soundtrack. The novel mentions three songs that are played at various moments in the story and, in this respect, the novel can be said to have background music. (Interestingly, the next book Esquivel published, *La ley del amor*, includes a music CD to be played at certain points in the story.) In the film of *Como agua* however, there is an orchestral soundtrack which was composed specifically for the film. This is most obvious during the opening credits and during the final love scene. Instruments (especially violins) are used to create tension, and to conjure up the mood in dramatic scenes, such as the magical-realist events. Nonetheless, the soundtrack contains six songs, three of which are the same ones as in the novel.

Most of the songs have a northern Mexican, or *norteña*, flavour, which is logical since they are the soundtrack for a film set on Mexico's northern border. Each plays a different role. 'Estrellita' is used for the serenade that the drunken Pedro and Juan Alejandrez sing to Tita — publicly declaring Pedro's love for Tita for the first time since his marriage to Rosaura. It is a song by Manuel Ponce, a composer from northern Mexico (Zacatecas). He and his music are significant because it is he who is considered to be the pioneer of Romantic musical nationalism (*30*, pp.124–29). This same notion of romantic nationalism could, in some ways, be applied to the book — a text steeped in romanticism and considered to be a celebration of Mexican life and customs. Ponce's song, written in 1912 and published in 1914, fits fairly well with the time frame of the narrative (though the action in *Como agua* takes place a little earlier).

The second song, 'Ojos de Juventud' is sung in the film by Rosaura on the morning after the night that she and Pedro finally consummate their marriage (several weeks after the wedding), though only the first line is sung. The initial impression is that it depicts Rosaura in a happy mood, as she quietly sings 'Ojos de juventud, puso en tu cara dios' to herself, but those who know the lyrics[16] will also catch the hidden message, as this is a song about betrayal, and the breaking of the beloved's heart. The melody and words give one of the few glimpses of events from Rosaura's perspective — a woman whose heart has been broken by someone with whom she has fallen in love.

If 'Ojos de Juventud' is a window into Rosaura's secrets and future, the third song, 'Jesusita in Chihuahua', plays a similar role for Gertrudis. It is at a party in the De la Garza home that we hear this lively Mexican folk song played (just music, no words), and we watch Gertrudis and Juan Alejandrez dance to it. As the whole room stops to watch the couple dance with great gusto, Rosaura speculates as to why it is that her sister dances so well, since, as she says, her mother did not like to dance and her father was a poor dancer. The narrative alludes to a stereotype that black people dance well because it is somehow in their blood. This is not the only time that this stereotype is mentioned (Gertrudis is also seen to detect a natural rhythm in the movement of kitchen utensils while they are preparing for Tita's birthday party), but the connection is always between rhythm and the African influence.

The fourth song, 'Mi querido capitán', is played at Esperanza's wedding feast, and is used to suggest the heightened sexual feelings that the guests are experiencing from the effects of the *chiles en nogada*. The song is clearly intended to express Gertrudis and Juan's dilemma, since the lyrics refer to a high-ranking military figure who

---

[16] Ojos de juventud puso en tu cara dios/volviendo a crear la luz eran para mi amor/como un rayo de sol de eterna plenitud. Ojos de juventud la vida mi me dio para llorar/para llorar tu amor que luego me engañó/con su traición vulgar. Ojos de juventud puso en tu cara dios/volviendo a crear la luz eran para mi amor/como una rayo de sol de eterna plenitud. (se repite lo anterior) Voy por la vida sin tu amor/como una ave sin final pues me rompiste el corazón/con tus manitas de marfil, como si fueran de cristal. Y como nunca de olvidar tu suprema ingratitud/ni tu traición.

falls in love. This is quite fitting, for both Juan and Gertrudis are ex-soldiers.

'Paso del Norte', the fifth song, is the one with the most melancholy melody: it is a *ranchera* and is played as the magical wedding cake is being dished out and eaten. Although it is about a man who goes north (to the USA) — something that will eventually happen to the De la Garza line as a result of the civil union — its specific purpose appears to be to evoke melancholy and nostalgia, which everyone feels as they eat the cake.

'Mi viejo carro Ford', the sixth song, is played on the radio and hints at the fact that a lot of time has passed since the previous scene, which left us wondering whether Tita would or would not marry John. The song refers to the passing of time, and to the modernisation that was sweeping the world at the time in the shape of the Ford motor car. This amusing song, which proclaims the woes of someone whose Ford has broken down, points to the new perils and frustrations which have arrived with modernity. It celebrates changing times and one of the inventions of the period — the motor car which all the De la Garza's elite circle of friends seem to own. The song is appropriate in that the car breaks down, and this could be interpreted as a kind of yearning for a pre-modern past. This is a yearning expressed by several people during Alex and Esperanza's wedding.

Sub-plots in the Film

Como agua has a number of sub-plots, created in the process of turning the novel into a film, and we can thus detect other stories within the main story. One of these smaller stories is that of Paquita Lobo. While she remains a minor character in both the book and the film, in the film we see that, as well as being the busybody of the novel, she has other secrets too.

In almost every scene in which she appears, Paquita Lobo is seen in the background, swapping gossip about the different families in the story. The name, Lobo, or wolf, is appropriate since she is often shown as involved in destroying another character's good name. When she is not guessing what is going on behind closed doors, she is sowing the seeds of doubt about people's character. An example of this is Paquita's conversation with another local woman as they enter the local church for Rosaura and Pedro's wedding. Not very discreetly, she tells her listener how surprised she is by the wedding, since it is common knowledge that Pedro and Tita are in love, and she relates how she has seen Tita give a perfumed letter to the groom just weeks before the wedding. She shares this piece of gossip while Tita and Gertrudis are within earshot. Paquita furthermore says that it is scandalous that the two will soon be living under the same roof. Thus, the film portrays Paquita as enjoying her role as the local scandalmonger. However, it is precisely during the wedding reception that we get the first hint that Paquita herself also enjoys an illicit love. As the narrator tells us about the magical qualities of the wedding cake, the camera focuses on Paquita, whose eyes are downcast while *she* appears to be remembering the love of *her* life. The camera then cuts to the priest, who too is suffering the strange intoxication caused by the cake. This appears to be an attempt to link the couple together, as if to suggest that they are the ones who are missing each other. There are other, later episodes, in which the background action between the two further suggests that Paquita has a romantic relationship with the priest.

During the *Rosa de Reyes* party, which is held in the De la Garza home, Chencha is the one to announce 'ya llegaron los metiches de los Lobo'. This caustic remark is not to be found in the book, thus allowing the film to further underline the way most people in the house feel about her. The same fiesta allows us to observe Paquita in action with the local priest. When Tita faints, the two characters to catch her are Paquita and the priest, sitting conveniently together. However, it is much later in the film, at Alex and Esperanza's wedding, that we discover that Paquita Lobo is not a busybody old maid but in fact, as we see on the wedding invitations, she is actually 'Doña Paquita Valdéz Vda. de Lobo', a connection which the film makes, but which is not made specific in the novel. At this wedding, apart from gossiping about how Rosaura would have loved to have been present (she is now dead), Paquita seems to disapprove of Tita's continuing to live on the ranch after Esperanza

moves away 'se vería muy mal' — while insinuating that something
might still be going on between the two of them. She even exposes
Mamá Elena's guilty secret, by saying in front of everyone just how
much Gertrudis dark-skinned daughter looks like her grandfather (the
mulatto). However, it is during this concluding episode that Paquita
herself is exposed as the priest's secret lover.

In a series of short clips of the wedding feast of *chiles en
nogada*, one of the couples seen eating the dish is the priest and
Paquita Lobo, who are wolfing down the chiles. Sexual innuendo is
clearly suggested when we see Paquita trying to stuff a whole 'chile'
into her mouth and the effects of the food cause the couples to run to
secret locations, to make love as soon as they can. In the frenzy to
leave, we see most of the main couples run hand in hand to find the
best (and closest) place to have sex. While everyone is seen
scattering, Paquita and the priest are holding hands in an easily
spotted position in the background, looking undecided as to where
their love nest should be. They run one way, then another —
allowing us to see that they are a couple — until finally leaving the
scene.

This small sub-plot allows for the development in the film of
minor characters in ways which were not possible in the novel.
Paquita's secret affair is gradually revealed to us. and this is not only
enjoyable — we can see the uncovering of Paquita's disreputable
secret — but it allows for some poetic justice, and some social
commentary on busybodies in small towns south of the Mexican
border.

Conclusion

In her essay on *Como agua*, Janice A. Jaffe describes the novel as a 'folletinesque love story' (7, p.208) and, in many ways, this is an accurate description. Given the unusual chapter divisions, splitting the book into months, and beginning with a recipe, it is clear that it follows the form of early novels such as *El Periquillo Sarniento*, which was originally published as a *folletín* or pamphlet. Seeing it as a novel in instalments allows us to understand why *Como agua* has chapters that describe events whose actions take place during months other than those which the chapter-titles would suggest. Similar in form to early womens' magazines, each section begins with a traditional recipe which is skilfully woven into the larger love story, spanning the twelve chapters. In theory, it provides one year of entertainment, to be given, just as the title promises, as 'entregas mensuales'.

Yet this is in appearance only, since the story is given to us not in instalments, but in its entirety, as a book which can be read quickly, and as film that can, if desired, be even more rapidly enjoyed. The intention of this brief study is to offer an overview of *Como agua*, with particular reference to the main themes and style. Those aspects which are unique to both the novel and the film have been examined, and we have seen that it is important to study both since they complement each other. We have noted that on some occasions the film expands and/or compresses the text of the novel. Some aspects, such as themes, are applicable to both; others, such as costumes and chiaroscuro, are unique to the film. Chapter structure — commented on above — refers only to the published version.

This critical guide is not to be viewed as a complete analysis of Esquivel's masterpiece, but rather as a text which will guide the reader through both the book and the film, increasing the under-standing of both, and provoking further study.

Bibliography

1. Britt, Linda. 'Translation, Criticism or Subversion? The Case of Like Water for Chocolate', *Translation Review*, 48–49 (1995), 10–14. This brief article studies the translation of *Como agua* and argues that in its translation from Spanish to English some of the 'magic' has been lost and that the English version of the text violates normal standards of reasonable translations.

2. Escaja, Tina. 'Reescribiendo a Penélope: mujer e identidad mejicana en *Como agua*', *Revista Iberoamericana*, 66 (2000), 571–86. This essay contemplates the role of humour and parody in *Como agua* while underlining the idea that this narrative effectively rewrites the archetypes of La Malinche, Guadalupe and Penelope.

3. Fox-Anderson, Catherine. 'Mysterium conjunctionis: la boda alquímica de Tita y Pedro en *Como agua: una novela de entregas mensuales con recetas, amores y remedios caseros*', *Explicación de textos literarios*, 29 (2001–2002), 92–103. Fox-Anderson's article incorporates some intriguing quotes and ideas in her article which links the love between the protagonists and death.

4. Giannotti, Janet. *A Companion Text for* Like Water for Chocolate (Ann Arbor: University of Michigan Press, 1999). This text is meant to aid school teachers in the teaching of this novel. While intended to create lesson plans, it also contains some additional information, such as historical information, activities, and images that can prove quite useful.

5. Hart, Stephen. '*Como agua*', *A companion to Latin American Film*, (Rochester: Tamesis, 2004), pp.171–78. This chapter provides and excellent summary of the film, much essential data, as well as offering critical comments with regard to the use of humour and magic realism.

6. Ibsen, Kristine. 'On Recipes, Reading and Revolution: Postboom Parody in *Como agua*', *Concerns*, 62 (1995), 133–46. This essay has some interesting ideas on the inversion of masculine and feminine roles in this narrative as well as considering this novel as a sort of denouncement of the *Manual de Carreño*.

7. Jaffe, Janice. 'Latin American Women Writer's Novel Recipes and Laura Esquivel's *Like Water for Chocolate*, *Scenes of the Apple: Food and the Female Body in 19th and 20th Century Women*, eds Tamar Heller and Patricia Moran (New York: Suny Press, 2003), pp.199–213.

This chapter considers the structure of the book and compares the twelve recipe chapters to twelve pamphlets, or folletínes, creating a serialized love story between Tita and Pedro. This author also makes links between writing and the kitchen.

8. Kaneko, Marie. 'A Resourceful Librarian's Tips for Starting a Collection', *Críticas Magazine* (2006), online resource www.criticasmagazine.com/article/CAG316428.html (consulted 2 June 2008), no pagination. This brief article makes mention of the rise of the Latin American film in the international arena and points to *Como agua* as the moment of its launch.

9. López-Rodríguez, Miriam. 'Cooking Mexicanness: Shaping National Identity in Alfonso Arau's *Como agua*', *Reel Food: Essays on Food and Film*, ed. Anne L. Bower (London: Routledge, 2004), pp.61–74. Miriam López-Rodríguez's essay studies the role of food in the film; considering it from historical, ethnic and socio-political vantage points as well as offering a feminist reading of the female characters in the film.

10. Madrid Moctezuma, Paola del Socorro. 'La epifanía de los cinco sentidos en dos ejemplos de narrativa femenina mexicana', *La literatura hispanoamericana con los cinco sentidos*, ed. Eva Valcarcel (A Coruña: Universidade da Coruña, 2002), pp.383–91. This chapter considers the role of food, sex, and our five senses in this narrative and a book of poetry by Martha Robles, *El celo de los deleites*. This brief study also makes mention of other literature in Latin America that makes significant use of food.

11. Marquet, Antonio. 'La receta de Laura Esquivel: ¿Cómo escribir un best-seller?', *Plural*, 237 (1991), 58–67. A rather early article on this novel, Marquet asks why Esquivel's novel was so popular and offers ideas as to what elements have made it so. It is a clear critique, but it does contain a few minor errors.

12. Martinez, Victoria. '*Como agua*: A Recipe for Neoliberalism', *Chasqui: Revista de Literatura Latinoamericana*, 33 (2004), 28–41. This article contains a brief, yet helpful, review of previous articles written on *Como agua*, as well as discussing characters in the narrative and their relation to food. The significance of the historical setting of the novel is also discussed.

13. McMahon, Donna. 'From the Kitchen to Eternity: The Feminine Voice in Laura Esquivel's *Like Water for Chocolate*', *Cine-Lit II*, eds George Cabello-Castellet and Jaume Marti-Olivella (Corvallis: Oregon State University, 1995), pp.19–28. This chapter compares Esquivel's novel to *Cien años de soledad* and considers issues of feminine identity with regard to some of the protagonists.

14. Monet-Viera, Molly. 'Post-Boom Magic realism: Appropriations and Transformations of a Genre', *Revista de Estudios Hispánicos*, 38

(2004), 95–117. *Como agua* is only one of the several narratives that
are part of a study on the role of magic realism in Latin American
literature. It argues that in Esquivel's novel the marvellous eclipses any
social realism the narrative might have.

15. Moreno, Ana Ibáñez. 'Análisis del mito de la madre terrible mediante
un estudio comparado de *La casa de Bernada Alba* y *Como agua*',
Espéculo, 32 (2006) (no pagination). True to its name, Moreno's article
uses Jung to analyse the myth of the over-dominant mother in two
novels. This comparative approach finds parallels in both the mother
and the daughters of the two works.

16. Niebylski, Dianna. 'Passion or Heartburn? The Uses of Humor in
Esquivel's and Arau's *Like Water for Chocolate*', *Literature and Film:
A Guide to the Theory and Practice of Film Adaptation*, eds Robert
Stam and Alessandra Raengo (Oxford: Blackwell Publishing, 2005),
pp.252–71. This article, which contains separate sections for both the
film and the book, argues that both the novel and the film are too
bourgeois and middle of the road to be truly revolutionary in their idea
of rewriting history.

17. Pérez, Alberto Julián. '*Como agua*: la nueva novella de mujeres en
Latinoamérica', *La nueva mujer en la escritura de autoras hispánicas:
ensayos críticos*, ed. Juana Arancibia (Westminster: Instituto Literario y
Cultura Hispánico, 1995), pp.41–58. Pérez places Esquivel in context
with her Latin American contemporaries and applies a femino-centric
critique to her first novel. This chapter has some worthwhile comments
with regards to magic realism and male-female role reversals in this
novel/film.

18. Potvin, Claudine. '*Como agua* ¿parodia o cliché?', *Revista Canadiense
de Estudios Hispánicos*, 20 (1995), 55–67. This essay views the film as
something which denies the female subject as having the ability to be
open, dynamic, multidimensional and capable of transforming
patriarchal order.

19. Price, Helene. 'Unsavoury Representations in Laura Esquivel's *Like
Water for Chocolate*', *A Companion to Magic Realism*, eds Stephen M.
Hart and Wen-chin Ouyang (Woodbridge: Tamesis, 2005), pp.181–90.
Dr Price argues that this narrative's huge success is due to its fast
flowing plot, love story, cookery book structure, and its inclusion of
magic. She believes that its magic defines its Mexican-ness but that
both productions fail to address real problems in Mexico.

20. Román-Odio, Clara. 'Clarividentes, Curanderas y Los Nuevos Rituales
De La Literatura Latinoamericana', *SECOLAS Annals: Journal of the
Southeastern Council on Latin American Studies*, 27 (1996), 41–48.
Román-Odio writes about spirituality and the role of the indigenous
woman in this narrative and demonstrates how Nacha, Chencha, and
Luz del Amanecer become spiritual guides/teachers for Tita.

21. Salkjelsvik, Kari. 'El desvío como norma: la retórica de la receta en *Como agua*', *Revista Iberoamericana*, 65 (1999), 171–182. Salkjelsvik analyses the structure and role of recipes within the novel, how they affect the composition of the book and how information is transmitted. This article also likens the *Manual de Carreño* to a recipe book for women's life within the narrative.

22. Saltz, Joanne. 'Laura Esquivel's *Como agua*: The Questioning of Literary and Social Limits', *Chasqui: Revista de Literatura Latinoamericana*, 24 (1995), 30–7. This article presents some ideas with regard to the characterization of Tita which are noteworthy (such as viewing her as the Virgin Mary), but it makes some errors with regard to some basic information in the narrative.

23. Segovia, Miguel. 'Only Cauldrons Know the Secrets of Their Soups, *Velvet Barrios: Popular Culture and Chicana/o Sexualities*', ed. Alicia Gaspar de Alba (New York: Palgrave Macmillan, 2003), pp.163–78. Segovia's text focuses on the characters in *Como agua* in a rather novel way; his essay argues that the novel upends binaries, reverses traditional gender roles and contains queer subtexts and queer cultural values.

24. Spina, Vincent. '"Useless Spaces" of the Feminine in Popular Culture: *Like Water for Chocolate* and *The Silent War*', *Imagination Beyond Nation: Latin American Popular Culture*', eds Eva P. Bueno and Terry Caesar (Pittsburgh: University of Pittsburgh Press, 1998), pp.210–26. This article compares the role of women in both texts and argues that they dismantle the traditional mythical woman. It has some interesting comments on the bathing ritual that exists between Mamá Elena and her daughter.

25. Valdés, María Elena. 'Verbal and Visual Representation of Women: *Como agua/Like Water for Chocolate*', *World Literature Today: A Literary Quarterly of the University of Oklahoma*, 69 (1995), 78–82. This article views both the film and the novel as a parody of early woman's magazines in Mexico and claims that while women would understand this film, men 'of any culture' would have a great 'deficiency in experiencing this film'.

26. Zamundio-Talyor, Victor and Inma Guiu. 'Criss-Crossing Texts: Reading Images in *Like Water for Chocolate*', *The Mexican Cinema Project*, ed. Chon Noriega (Los Angeles: UCLA, 1995), pp.46–56. This article argues that *Como agua* was and is popular due to the fact that many different voices are heard in the narrative. There are a lot of interesting comments with regard to the filming of the film version of this novel.

27. Zubiaurre, Maite. 'Culinary Eros in Contemporary Hispanic Female Fiction: From Kitchen Tales to Table Narratives', *College Literature*, 33 (2006), 29–51. This article focuses on the role food and women in

Como agua and draws interesting parallels with other similar narratives in recent Latin American literature.

Other cited works

28. 'Alfonso Arau', *IMDb*, 2008, online database, www.imdb.com/name/nm0000778 (consulted 25 November 2008), no pagination.

29. Arora, Shirley. *Proverbial Comparisons and Related Expressions in Spanish* (Berkeley: University of California Press, 1977).

30. Béhague, Gerard. *Music in Latin America; an Introduction* (Englewood Cliffs: Prentice Hall Inc, 1979).

31. Brading, David. *Mexican Phoenix: Our Lady of Guadalupe: Image and Tradition Across Five Centuries* (Cambridge: Cambridge University Press, 2001).

32. Camargo-Ricalde, Sara L. and Grether, Rosaura. 'Germinación, dispersión y establecimiento de plántulas de Mimosa tenuiflora (Leguminosae) en México', *Revista de Biología Tropical,* 46 (1998), 543–554.

33. Chang-Rodríguez, Raquel and Malva E. Filer. *Voces de Hispanoamérica* (Boston: Heinle, 2004).

34. García Márquez, Gabriel. *Cien años de soledad* (Madrid: Real Academia Española y Alfaguara, 2007).

35. Gonzalbo Aizpuru, Pilar. *Las mujeres en la nueva España* (Mexico City: Colegio de México, 1987).

36. Guenther, Irene. 'Magic Realism in the Weimer Republic', *Magic Realism: Theory, History, Community*, eds Lois Parkinson Zamora and Wendy B. Faris (London: Duke University Press, 1995), pp.33–73.

37. Hidalgo, Margarita. *Perceptions of Spanish-English Code-Switching in Júarez, Mexico* (Albuquerque: University of New Mexico, 1988).

38. Jones, Adam. 'Los muertos de Cuidad Júarez', *Letras Libres,* 64 (2004), 36–38.

39. Katz, Fredrich. *The Life and Times of Pancho Villa* (Stanford: Stanford University Press, 1998).

40. Knight, Alan. 'Racism, Revolution, and Indigenismo: Mexico, 1910– 1940', *The Idea of Race in Latin America, 1870–1940*, ed. Richard Graham (Austin: University of Texas Press, 1990), pp. 71–113.

41. Latorre, Felipe. *The Mexican Kickapoo Indians* (Austin: Courier Dover Publications, 1991).

42. Lauwers, Judith and Swisher, Anna. *Counseling the Nursing Mother* (London: Jones & Bartlett Publishers, 2005).

43. Pavlovski, Linda. 'Magic Realism: Introduction', *Twentieth-Century Literary Criticism*, ed. Linda Pavlovski, Gale Group (2001), online

resource www.enotes.com/twentieth-century-criticism/magicrealism (consulted 23 June 2008), no pagination.

44. Salas, Elizabeth. *Soldaderas in the Mexican Military: Myth and History* (Austin: University of Texas Press, 1990).
45. Smith, Joan. 'Laura Esquivel on *Like Water for Chocolate*, Destiny and The Thoughts of Inanimate Objects', Salon (1996), online magazine www.salon.com/oct96/interview2961104.html (consulted 19 November 2008), no pagination.
46. Summers, Elspeth and Andrew Holms (eds), *Collins English Dictionary* (Glasgow: Harper Collins Publishers, 2006).
47. Stern, Alexandra Minna. 'From Mestizophilia to Biotypology', *Race and Nation in Modern Latin America*, eds Nancy P. Appelbaum, Anne S. Macpherson, and Karin Alejandra Rosenblatt (Chapel Hill: University of North Carolina Press, 2003), pp. 187–210.
48. Tripp, Edward. *Dictionary of Classical Mythology* (Glasgow: Collins Publishers, 1970).
49. Vaughn, Mary. 'Women, Class, and Education in Mexico, 1880–1928', *Women in Latin America* (Riverside: Latin American Perspectives, 1979), pp. 63–80.

Other books by Laura Esquivel

La ley del amor (1995)
Íntimas suculencias (1998)
Estrellita marinera (1999)
El libro de las emociones (2000)
Tan veloz como el deseo (2001)
Malinche (2006)